Militants for

Jesus Christ

JANICE H. HICKS

Publisher's Name: Janice H. Hicks

ISBN: 978-1-968442-95-8

eBook ISBN: 978-1-968442-96-5

Faith at Its Finest

Not too long ago, I came upon a Marine's Bible. The Bible had engraved "United States Marine Corps" on the front of its leather cover in gold, printed by Holman Christian Standard Bible.

I'd never seen a military Bible before especially printed for a branch of a military service. I want to share with you, my readers, the brave hearts of the people who serve and protect our country as they shared their prayers in the Marine's Bible.

Their dedication and faith put into action on the front line of battle in real time is something that awed me. How it takes trust in a God mightier themselves to fight and to risk their very lives to keep and to protect our country from the bondage of communism and the threat of losing the freedom that we embrace and hold so dear today. The freedom and liberty to worship a true and loving God. To keep us from dictators and tyranny and false gods.

These Christian soldiers included in the Marine's Bible, their prayers to encourage us all. Here are some of those prayers. I hope that their prayers and faith in the might and glory of a true living God in action encourages you as it has me. Amen.

How Should a Warrior Pray?
By Col. Don Martin, USA (Retired)

In time of war, how should a warrior pray?

After the death of Moses, Joshua led Israel to besiege Jericho. As he approached the city, an armed figure stood in his way. Joshua's natural response was to demand, "Are you for us or for our enemies?" "Neither," he replied. "I have now come as commander of the Lord's army."

"Remove the sandals from your feet, for the place where you are standing is holy." And Joshua did so (Josh. 5: 13–15).

In like manner, Christian warriors today should not focus on the question: Is God on our side? Instead, they should test their attitudes and actions with the question: Am I serving the Lord and praying in obedience to Jesus Christ?

What fundamentals and themes of prayer should a Christian warrior focus on when war comes? A response limited to one page in *command* can't be exhaustive. It can, however, offer a starting point for warriors who long to pray effectively and for those who love them and support in prayer.

A Warrior's Perspective

Continually give thanks that, spiritually, you are seated with Christ in the heavens (Eph. 2:4–7). Keep focused on the Lord Jesus and on his power to lead and assist you. Give him praise and glory in every circumstance of your life.

Pray for a biblical understanding of your duty as an agent of human government. Chapters 12 and 13 of Romans provide clear directions. Do not seek to punish others for personal wrongs done to you. Instead, obey human rulers who are fulfilling the God-given obligation of suppressing evil deeds and punishing those who commit them. Ask God to grant you confidence and strength in your role as an obedient servant of the American people, as you execute the legal orders of those who have been elected to lead our nation in a conflict with evildoers.

Pray that God will conform your character into the character of Jesus Christ. This is his eternal purpose for you (Rom. 8:29). The reason why "all things work together for the good" is that God uses them to fulfill his intent to make you like his Son. Pray that he will do so in these days.

Pray that Jesus Christ will be exalted and that God's purposes for the nations, peoples, and tribes of the world will be fulfilled. The God who created the universe and who sustains it by his word of power was not surprised by the attacks of these terrorists. Ask him to display his holiness, majesty, power, love, mercy, and righteous judgment to all peoples throughout the world.

A Warriors Preparation

Ask God to teach you to become more effective in prayer. Study the Scripture and learn to pray using biblical content or passages from the Bible.

Ask God to teach you how to "pray constantly" (1 Thess. 5:17). Take advantage of brief moments throughout the day when you can praise and thank God or ask for his divine help for yourself and others. When the OPTEMPO is intense, brief prayers interspersed throughout your duty day may offer the best opportunity for effective communion with the Lord. Decide that you will pray even though "there is no time to pray."

On Alert
By Lt. Col. Ward Graham, USAF (Retired)

Today is a time of rich opportunity for Christians in the military—a time that calls forth the warrior spirit in the followers of Christ. As an officer said to me recently, "Are we warriors or are we to find safe havens where our lives will be comfortable and secure?"

What is your answer to that question? Mine was to recall some of the warnings and injunctions of the New Testament. Jesus told his followers to be ready for times like these when there would be "wars and rumors of wars. See that you are not alarmed because these things must take place, but the end is not yet. For nation will rise up against nation, and kingdom against kingdom" (Matt. 24: 6–7).

He also told them to be alert for such times. "Watch! Be alert! For you don't know when the time is coming. Therefore, be alert since you don't know when the master of the house is coming…he might come suddenly and find you sleeping. And what I say to you, I say to everyone: be alert" (Mark 13:33, 35–37).

Are we on alert? *Are we warriors ready for spiritual battle and available to the master's call to spiritual action?* While Jesus may have been speaking of his return, the principle of alertness applies to us all in every generation and circumstance.

I spent seven years of my life "sitting alert" in the air force. For part of that time, I was a "good guy" piloting an air defense fighter in protection of US assets at home and abroad. Later I was a "bad guy" manning a nuclear bomber ready to wreak destruction upon the enemies of. In both situations, I was required to hold myself required to hold myself ready for an immediate launch at the sound of the trumpet. Many times I scrambled into the air in minutes to fight off an attacking bomber or race out to the runway ready to launch with weapons of mass destruction. I know what Jesus means when he says, "Be on the alert."

Later, as a Christian officer, I applied some of lessons of sitting alert to the people and circumstances of military life. New friends in the body of Christ trained me to be prepared with a ready explanation of the gospel for those opportunities I could create, or which came my way.

Are you similarly sitting alert with the good news of Christ's redemptive plan? Are you prepared to pay the price for standing up for his Name and his moral instructions for man?

The Apostle Paul surely knew how to make the most of opportunities to do battle in any and all circumstances. Do you remember his memorable return to Jerusalem recorded in Acts 21–22? In the midst of his worship in the temple area, he was arrested and dragged from those hallowed grounds, and the gate was slammed shut behind him. His accusers then tried to kill him.

A Roman commander became aware of the riot and, taking a contingent of officers and men, proceeded to break up the melee and to rescue Paul. The violence was so heated, the soldiers had to physically jilt Paul above the crowd as they took him toward the barracks. When they reached the stairs, Paul procured permission from the commander to address the crowd below. In a similar circumstance, what would you have done? What would you have said? The bloody, battered, and bruised Paul chose to ignore the hatred of his adversar- ies. Instead, he spoke a message of the love of God in Jesus Christ.

Can you picture yourself turning such adversity into an opportunity to witness to your accusers? This is what the Christian life is all about— turning adversity into a message of love. The committed Christian will see much trouble and adversity in his lifetime as Paul explained in 2 Timothy 3:12, saying "In fact, all those who want to live godly life in Christ Jesus will be persecuted." Jesus explained that the world would hate him and his friends (1 John 15:18–20). His close follower, John, perhaps echoing Jesus's teaching, said, "Do not be surprised, brothers, if the world hates you" (1 John 3:13).

What is the role of the OCF warrior in times like these? We describe it by what we call the OCF strategy, which is composed of the OCF purpose, pillars, and vision statement. Are you familiar with them? The OCF council and staff would like you to know and understand these because they are the battle plan by which the Holy Spirit is guiding our warfare in enemy territory.

The OCF purpose is to glorify God by uniting Christian offi- cers for biblical fellowship and outreach, equipping and encourag- ing them to minister effectively in the military. Historically, OCF (Officers'

Christian Fellowship) has sought to accomplish this calling of God by what we know as the Spiritual Pillars of OCF.

We seek to:

- Be a lay movement within the services to which called.
- Center on Scripture individually and corporately.
- Engage in prayer, which shows our dependence upon God.
- Unite for fellowship, for encouragement, and mutual strengthening.
- Equip to serve so that we may be effective warriors in our units.
- Integrate to serve, for encouragement and mutual strengthening.
- Nurture military families.
- Support and encourage chaplains.

While we do the ordinary, everyday work to which God has called us (purpose and pillars), we call out to God to accomplish as extraordinary work in the military and the nation. This we call the OCF vision, which is a spiritually transformed military with ambassadors for Christ in uniform, empowered by the Holy Spirit, living with a passion for God and compassion for the entire military society.

This vision has led us to ask our members and friends to join us in praying for revival in the military and our nation. This has been the purpose of the Sound the Trumpet weekend gatherings and other prayer vigils.

Are we willing to be identified with Jesus no matter what the cost? This is a time to be bold for Jesus and to seize the moment afforded us by the great turmoil in our nation and military and to proclaim the liberating. The work of Jesus is calling his warriors, his ambassadors in uniform. Are you answering the call?

The purpose of Officers' Christian Fellowship is to glorify God by uniting Christian officers for biblical fellowship and outreach, equipping and encouraging them to minister effectively in the military.

Local OCF fellowships are composed of all ranks from cadets and midshipmen to senior officers and retirees.

Officers' Christian Fellowship desires to serve those who serve their country. They have a number of resources to help military members and their families grow together in their relationship with God and others.

In 1997, Lt. Col Ward G. Graham, USAF (Retired) became a member of the Officers' Christian Fellowship staff and serves as the OCF staff representative for the East Central region of the USA. The lieutenant colonel travels with his wife, Bobbe, to military installations and ROTC schools. He served in the USA Air Force from 1952–1973.

To all military personnel, past and present, thank you for your service. Officers' Christian Fellowship https://www.ocfusa.org/

2 Timothy 3:16–17; 1; P. 1: 20–21.

All scripture is given by inspiration of God and is profitable for doctrine, for reproof, for correction, for instruction in righteousness. That the man of God may be perfect and thoroughly furnished unto all good works.

Above all, you must understand that no prophecy of scripture came about by the prophet's own interpretation of things. For proph- ecy never had its origin in the human will, but prophets, though human, spoke from God as they were carried along by the Holy Spirit. Amen.

FYI, so as not to cause indifference toward women of God, or to exclude myself as a woman of God, and to help us not completely focus the gift of prophesy entirely, and literally, to men only (as some have erroneously done), please allow me to introduce you to my sisters of old who paved the way for us and to show that God will use who he will for the furtherance of his kingdom, and he proves that he truly is no respecter of person. And in his kingdom, the kingdom of heaven, there is no male or female.

"There can be neither Jew nor Greek, there can be neither bond nor free, there can be no male and female; for ye all are one, in Christ Jesus" (Gal. 3:28). If God said it, I believe it, and that settles it. Scripture also tells us to let God be true and every man a liar. We are to be obedient to the call of God and follow the leading of the Holy Spirit.

"God forbid yea, let God be true, but every man a liar; as it is written, that thou mightest be justified in thy sayings, and mightest overcome when thou art judged" (Rom. 3:4). Amen. Let there be no division among us because a house divided against itself cannot stand. We need one another to finish our purpose and to complete our courses. To run this race, we must stand together as one as our Father is one in Christ Jesus our Lord and Savior, the Messiah.

Let us rightly divide the scripture, for in them we think we may have life. "Search the scriptures; for in them ye think ye have eternal life: and they are they which testify of me" (John 5:39).

Let me start with Mary Magdalene, where she is known as an Apostle of Jesus Christ, according to authors Karen L. King, author of *The Gospel of Mary of Magdala: Jesus and the First Woman Apostle*, and the *Gospel of Mary Magdalene* author, Jean-Yves Leloup. She is considered to be a saint by some.

I like to start with her because she played a pivotal part in the establishment of the early Christian church and in being the very first person that the risen Christ appeared to (Mark 16:9). Now when Jesus was risen early the first day of the week, he appeared first to Mary Magdalene, out of whom he had cast seven devils. And he told her to spread the good news of the resurrected Christ to the Apostles and the disciples.

It was Jesus Christ himself who called her by name and assigned her this assignment in Mark 16:11–18.

> But Mary stood without at the sepulcher weeping: and as she wept, she stooped down, *and looked* into the sepulcher, and seeth two angels in white sitting, the one at the head, and the other at the feet, where the body of Jesus had lain. And they say unto her, "Woman, why weepest thou?" She saith unto them, "Because they have taken away my Lord, and I know not where they have laid him."

> And when she had thus said, she turned her- self back, and saw Jesus standing, and knew not that it was Jesus. Jesus saith unto her, "Woman, why weepest thou? Whom seekest thou?" She, supposing him to be the gardener, saith unto him, "Sir, if thou have borne him hence, tell me where thou hast laid him, and I will take him away."

> Jesus saith unto her, "Mary." She turned herself, and saith unto him, "Rabboni," which is to say, "Master." Jesus saith unto her, "Touch me not; for I am not yet ascended to my Father: but go to my brethren, and say unto them, I ascend unto my Father, and your Father; and *to* my God, and your God." Mary Magdalene came and told the disciples that she had seen the Lord, and *that* he had spoken these things unto her.

Mary Magdalene followed Jesus closely during his three-year

ministry. He validated her position in the kingdom of God: "My father and your father, my God, and your God." She is mentioned by name twelve times in the canonical gospels, more than most of the apostles and more than any other woman in the gospels, other than Jesus's family. Because she was the first to witness Jesus's resurrection, Mary Magdalene is known in some Christian traditions as the "apostle to the apostles."

She is a central figure in later Gnostic Christian writings, including the Dialogue of the Savior, the *Pistis Sophia*, the Gospel of Thomas, the Gospel of Philip, and the Gospel of Mary. These texts portray her as an apostle, as Jesus's closest and most beloved disciple, and the only one who truly understood his teachings.

The definition of an *apostle* (from the Greek *apostolos*) is "one who is sent" or "one commissioned." The term (pronounced *uh-pos-ull*) appears more than eighty times in the New Testament. In Hebrews 3:1, the word was applied to Jesus Christ, who was sent by God. The qualifications of this type of apostle were: (1) to have been a witness of the resurrected Christ (1 Cor. 9:1), (2) to have been explicitly chosen by the Holy Spirit (Acts 9:15), and (3) to have the ability to perform signs and wonders (Acts 2:43; 2 Cor. 12:12).

Miriam is referenced in the Bible as a prophetess and was the daughter of Amram, the leader of the Israelites in ancient Egypt, and of Jochebed, and the sister of Aaron and Moses. She is called "Miriam the prophetess" in Exodus 15:20, and Miriam the prophetess, the sister of Aaron.

In the Book of Judges, Deborah was a prophetess ("And Deborah, a prophetess, the wife of Lapidoth, she judged Israel at that time" [Judg. 4:4]), of the God of the Israelites, the fourth judge of pre-monarchic Israel, and the only female judge mentioned in the Bible.

I love queen Esther's courage: "She said if I die let me did" (Esther 4:16). A man named Haman had devised a plan to destroy the Jews held in bondage in Persia. Queen Esther's cousin,

Mordecai, encouraged her to go before the king at a time that's not her designated time.

He had learned of the plot to destroy his people by Haman and told Esther about it and asked her to go before the king and he said, "For if thou altogether holdest thy peace at this time, *then* shall there enlargement and deliverance arise to the Jews from another place; but thou and thy father's house shall be destroyed: and who knoweth whether thou art come to the kingdom for *such* a time as this?" (Esther 4:14).

She consented to the plan of Mordecai and said, "If I perish, I perish!" She girded her strength and called for a fast and went before the king and favor was granted, and that evil plan that Haman planned against Mordecai and the people of God was turned on him. Jael, a woman in the Book of Judges in the Old Testament during the time of Deborah, was the prophetess and judge of Israel who prophesized the honor would go to a woman for defeating Jabin's army. Here's Jael's story from Judges 4:

> And Deborah, a prophetess, the wife of Lapidoth, she judged Israel at that time.

> And she dwelt under the palm tree of Deborah between Ramah and Bethel in mount Ephraim: and the children of Israel came up to her for judgment. And she sent and called Barak the son of Abinoam out of Kedeshnaphtali, and said unto him, "Hath not the Lord God of Israel commanded, saying, 'Go and draw toward mount Tabor, and take with thee ten thousand men of the children of Naphtali and of the children of Zebulun? And I will draw unto thee to the river Kishon Sisera, the captain of Jabin's army, with his chariots and his multitude; and I will deliver him into thine hand.'

And Barak said unto her, "If thou wilt go with me, then I will go: but if thou wilt not go with me, then I will not go."

And she said, "I will surely go with thee: notwithstanding the journey that thou tak- est shall not be for thine honour; for the Lord shall sell Sisera into the hand of a woman." And Deborah arose and went with Barak to Kedesh. And Jael went out to meet Sisera, and said unto him, "Turn in, my lord, turn in to me, fear not." And when he had turned in unto her into the tent, she covered him with a mantle.

And he said unto her, "Give me, I pray thee, a little water to drink; for I am thirsty." And she opened a bottle of milk, gave him drink, and cov- ered him.

Again he said unto her, "Stand in the door of the tent, and it shall be, when any man doth come and enquire of thee, and say, is there any man here? That thou shalt say no."

Then Jael Heber's wife took a nail of the tent, and took a hammer in her hand, and went softly unto him, and smote the nail into his tem- ples, and fastened it into the ground: for he was fast asleep and weary. So he died.

And behold, as Barak pursued Sisera, Jael came out to meet him, and said unto him, "Come, and I will shew thee the man whom thou seekest." And when he came into her tent, behold, Sisera lay dead, and the nail was in his temples.

Wow. What a story to read about the conquests and the plights of the women who our Lord called and used for his purpose, honor, and glory. There are some of TV's series, *CSI*, *Forensic Files*, and *Bones*, that describe crimes scene investigations detailing things like fingerprint analysis, hair analysis, DNA, and blood splatter.

I can visualize Jael having blood in her face, on her clothes, obviously on Sisera himself, and on her hands because the force and impact with which she plunged the stake or peg into the skull of Sisera went cleaned through to the ground. Probably on the tent's ceiling too. The force with which she had to have used to strike with the intent and drive that went through her to accomplish her purpose.

With the blood splatter cases, pictures are taken of the surfaces found at the scenes to help determine how the victims were killed, with what type of a weapon may have been used to commit the crimes. And yes, there are blood vessels in the temple region where Jael struck Sisera in otherwise known as the forehead. The temporal arteries, which supply blood from the heart to the scalp, are located near the temples and can be felt as a pulse.

Jael is said to have used a tent peg as a nail to kill Sisera because it's assumed that she was strong and skilled in using a mallet and tent peg, which were the elements of repairing and pitching tents in biblical times.

Jael's dexterity in handling the hammer and stake probably had to do with the fact that it was usually the women's job to set up and dismantle the tents.

Deborah and Jael is a biblical history that is renewed even today and was even portrayed in *Law & Order*'s sixth season episode "Pro Se," where the main suspect suffers from delusions—evoked by his diagnosed schizophrenia—that he is Sisera and is paranoid about women being Jael. *The Cross and the Tent Peg: How Jesus Retraced*

Jael's Story by Julie Walsh (Regent University) is an eye-opening work of diligent, careful, meticulous, and thorough study, drawing on a wealth of existing literature and distinguished by an astute, original analysis of biblical verses. By demonstrating that Jesus saw a woman's action as having significance for his own death, Walsh raises crucial questions about the traditional roles of women in the family, in society, and within the church.

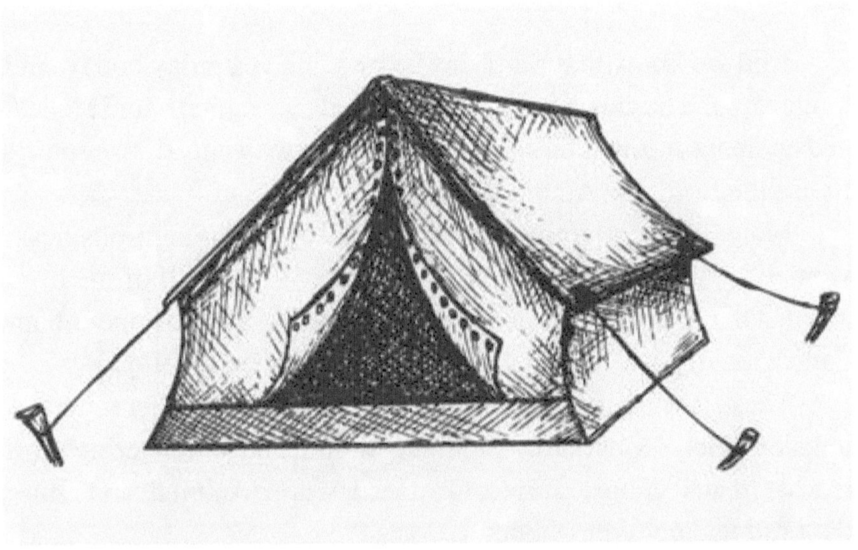

The Song of Deborah (Judges 5:24–26) recounts:

Extolled above women be Jael,
Extolled above women in the tent.
He asked for water, she gave him milk;
She brought him cream in a lordly dish.
She stretched forth her hand to the nail,
Her right hand to the workman's hammer,
And she smote Sisera; she crushed his head,
She crashed through and transfixed his temples.

And we know that our Lord is the same yesterday, today, and tomorrow and he changes not. He respected the women of old biblical and ancient time, and he still does today in the twenty-first century. Praise the Lord and Amen.

Many of the women of God were very prominent business-women in their time and chosen vessels to do the will of the Lord and that they did as we do as well today, to the glory and honor of our Father, leaving us a faithful legacy to embrace and to follow.

These women support scriptures that there is neither male nor female in God's kingdom. A willing, faithful, and surrendering heart is what he will choose. Amen. Go ahead, women of God, and praise the Lord and get your shout on!

Copy and paste this to your browser to access the link: https://youtu.be/ShdI2k5kCAk.

Copy and paste this to your browser to access the link: https://youtu.be/rrBhchgIGbY?si=fmZH_Tst2ffiZwrn.

Be encouraged to hold on with these videos from Mississippi Mass Choir with guest Walter Hawkins and The Caravans, respectfully.

An old Christian hymnal, "Walking up the King's Highway (It's a Highway to Heaven)" by Mary Gardner and Dr. Thomas A. Dorsey:

> It's a highway to heaven
> None can walk up there
> But the pure in heart
> Walking up the King's highway
> It's a highway to heaven
> None can walk up there.
> But the pure in heart
> Walking up the King's highway

Chapter One

Militants for Christ Jesus

In the *Merriam-Webster Dictionary*, the word *militant* is an adjective that means "engaged in warfare or combat, or aggressively active in a cause." It can also be a noun that means "militant protesters" or "militant attitude."

Growing up and well into my adulthood, the word *militant* was used to describe a person whose almost always carried a negative connotation. Even in the church, some ministers and some evangelists were given the cold shoulder, and some were distanced and standoffish from the other preachers if they were thought to be *too militant* in their deliverance of a sermon.

I was a new member at my present church some years ago, and there was a powerful preacher there who was not only a powerful man of God and intimidating in appearance being approximately around six feet and four inches in height and weighed somewhere around 300 pounds in weight, but also in his deliverance of a message and when he would pound the podium with his hand when the anointing was strong on him. I personally didn't believe it was out of anger as some would say, but I just thought it was his imposing size and that it could easily be misinterpreted as anger.

Me, I was absolutely mesmerized and somewhat afraid too because he showed that the Lord was to be revered, honored, and worshipped. He preached the unadulterated Word without an opinionated twist or compromise. I'll always remember this man of God for preaching the Word with fear and trembling of God and not being moved be the fear of the stares of the condescending stares from some of the congregation.

It's in my opinion that he was just a *militant* for his Lord, Jesus Christ. He was judged by his performance of the Word, "Why does he have talk so loud, why does he have to pound on the podium so hard?"

I have an answer to those questions, and it's because he was passionate about the ministry and Word of God, of the contents of God's Word. What a shame, because for some, what he preached just went over their heads and not into their spirit and heart and soul because they allowed their carnal minds to distract them from the salvation of their heart's minds and soul. "Because the carnal mind is enmity against God" (Rom. 8:7).

Jesus said, "And from the days of John the Baptist until now the kingdom of heaven suffereth violence, and the violent take it by force" (Matt. 11:12).

It was John the Baptist who ushered in the new covenant through King Jesus Christ when he said, "He it is, who coming after me is preferred before me, whose shoe's latchet I am not worthy to unloose" (John 1:27).

The kingdom of heaven is a spiritual realm. The term kingdom of God is interchangeable with the kingdom of heaven, and within this kingdom, there is only one God and one Lord of us all, ruler of all, Jesus Christ the son of God. The Creator of all things. I like to look at this scripture in comparison or parallel with the rebellion that took place within God's heavenly kingdom in the Book of Genesis, "And there was war in heaven: Michael and his angels fought against the dragon; and the dragon fought and his angels. And prevailed not neither was their place found any more in heaven" (Rev. 12:7–8).

We're fighting that same adversary and the same dragon, and that same war continues from heaven on earth today, make no mistake about it. The enemy whose only purpose is to steal, kill, and to destroy those who shall inherit the kingdom of heaven, the joint heirs with Christ, that being the anti-Christ, Satan the devil.

"And it was given to him *to make war* with the saints, and to overcome them: and power was given him over all kindreds, and tongues, and nations. *And all that dwell on the earth* shall worship him, *whose names are not written in the book of life of the Lamb slain from the foundation of the world* (Rev. 13:7–8). So, yes, this is a continuation of the war in heaven in the Book of Genesis.

For we fight not against flesh and blood but against powers and principalities and spiritual wickedness in high places. Truly, the kingdom of heaven suffereth violence and the violent taketh by force. But the battle is not ours; it's the Lord's, and we know that we have an expected end.

> "For I know the plans I have for you," declares
> the Lord, "plans to prosper you and not to harm you,
> plans to give you hope and a future." (Jer. 29:11)

> If we suffer, we shall also reign with him, if we
> deny him, he also will deny us. (2 Tim. 2:12)

I am that militant for Christ Jesus and my Savior. Having on the whole armor of God wherewith, I'm battle ready and fully equipped to resist the wiles of Satan. My faith, my trust, my hope, and my confidence are not in my own abilities, but it's in none other than my ever-present help in the times of trouble, Jesus Christ, the Anointed One and my personal friend (Ps. 46:1).

Let us be careful and *alert* that we pick and choose our battles wisely. I learned that sound advice some time ago. We are given freedom to choose in life, whether to do right or to do bad. My choice is to fight the good fight of faith for my soul salvation.

https://youtu.be/4q-foYz0Ek4?si=N-HMdLWuEpaxRAAK

I will "PRESS" even when it hurt even when it hurts even when I'm in distress by Maranda Curtis.

https://youtu.be/sIaT8Jl2zpI?si=cOE9LZLzWpGdMESR "You Say" by Lauren Daigle.

I have come too far to turn around now. He's sweeter today than he was yesterday.

Notes

Chapter Two

Angel Assistance

I can attest to the existence of angels in my personal life. The Bible is very real in every aspect of its existence. First, as a very young girl, somewhere around the ages of ten to twelve years old, I had experienced a horrible incident that traumatized my life for a very long time. Because of that traumatic experience I started to be in fear of the dark.

One night, fear gripped me to the point where I was totally petrified to the point of numbness, crouched in between a very narrow wall and a small bookcase in my bedroom, just paralyzed with the spirit of fear. I had a loss of speech and movement. Suddenly, angels appeared, maybe four of them, who walked toward me and picking a part of me up and taking me away in the spirit as I watched them until they disappeared. I watched me in their custody, which now believe was a tormenting spirit derived from the enemy originating from an intended lesson imposed upon me from a teacher, and I went to bed to never experience that fear again.

I am a witness to those guardian angels given charge to keep the saved ones in Christ Jesus. He was my ever-present help in my time of trouble. Another experience is a near-drowning experience where the servants of God lifted me above the surface to safety. It was as though the hands of angels were pushing me high and lifted up and to that surface of survival. I'd like to mention that at neither of these instances was I fearful or afraid. I was left with nothing but calmness and peace that totally embraced me. Amen.

For he shall give his angels charge over thee, to keep thee in all thy ways. They shall bear thee up in their hands, lest thou dash thy foot against a stone. Thou shalt tread upon the lion and adder: the young lion and the dragon shalt thou trample under feet. Because he hath set his love upon me, therefore will I deliver him: I will set him on high, because he hath known my name. He shall call upon me, and I will answer him: I will be with him in trouble; I will deliver him and honor him. With long life will I satisfy him and show him my salvation. (Ps. 91:11–16)

But to which of the angels said he at any time, sit on my right hand, until I make thine enemies thy footstool? Are they not all minister- ing spirits, sent forth to minister for them who shall be heirs of salvation? (Heb. 1:13–14)

So the next time the enemies of the cross and that ole anti- Christ, the devil, asks, "You and what army?" With confidence and boldness, declare and decree, with boldness and Holy Ghost power within you, "Me and the army of the Lord, Jesus Christ." Know that you are that one who can put a thousand to flight. Amen.

Notes

Chapter Three

Houses Divided

I am so glad that I stumbled upon the Marine's Bible because it reveals the hearts and the intents of the men on the battlefield in real time. Who fight for God and country that we Americans live in freedom and liberty. Who shared with us their personal testimonies and their faith that they have in the One, True, and Living God. How they've trusted him fearlessly to lead them and to direct their paths in every way.

Which is why I've included excerpts for hope in providing you, my readers, with the examples and the advice these men boldly gave to us, the believers of Christ Jesus, on how we're to live this life of faith believing that we can make it and will make it to the end.

I think it's an honorable calling and ministry of God for those in military working together to teach other soldiers the faith and biblical principles to live by and the comradery of fellowship that was created for and among themselves.

That is what it looks like in the kingdom of God and his righteousness, and I am so thankful and grateful for this ministry. For as the scripture reads in Ephesians 4:5–6, "One Lord, one faith, one baptism, One God and Father of all, who is above all, and through all, and in you all."

Paul said, "Follow me as I follow Christ" (1 Cor. 11:1), and he had this confidence that he would see the Lord in peace (2 Tim. 4:7–8). He said I have fought a good fight, I have finished the race, and I have kept the faith. Finally, there is laid up for me the crown of righteousness, which the Lord, the Righteous Judge, will give to me on that day, and not to me only but also to all who have loved his appearing: and that's why we live this life so that we will receive eternal life with Christ Jesus our Savior and Redeemer.

Hebrews 2:3–4: "How shall we escape, if we neglect so great salvation, which at the first began to be spoken by the Lord and was confirmed unto us by them that heard him. God also bearing them witness, both with signs and wonders, and with divers miracles, and gifts of the Holy Ghost, according to his own will?"

Indeed, because we read the scripture of our Savior in the Garden of Gethsemane: "Then Jesus came with them to a place called Gethsemane" (Matt. 26:36). In verse 39, he went a little farther and fell on his face and prayed, saying, "O my Father, if it is possible, let this cup pass from me; nevertheless, not as I will, but as you will."

And elsewhere the scripture tells us that Jesus said, "No man taketh it from me, but I lay it down of myself. I have power to lay it down, and I have power to take it again. This commandment have I received of my Father" (John 10:17–18).

What a mighty God we serve. He prevailed the cross from the heart of unconditional love for you and me. He became the perfect sacrifice, a lamb without spot or blemish, and offered himself a blood sacrifice because without the shedding of blood, there can be no forgiveness of sins. And while we were yet in our sins, he died for us that all who love, worship, serve, obey, and trust in him shall have eternal life. And after three days, he rose again with all power in his hands and set down on the right hand of God.

The Bible teaches us that a house divided against itself *shall not stand* (Mark 3:25). Consider the Old Testament scripture of the Tower of Babel, what it looks like to be of singleness of mind. Though their intentions and purpose were evil, they were going to achieve what they set out to do, unless they were stopped.

Not haphazardly but with the precision of master builders. I can envision that there were graphic designs, architectural designs, sculptures, brick layers, painters, and masonry builders all working together to finish this massive structure.

There had to have been foremen, supervisors, managements of up and lower levels, authorities, and other authorities and rulers directing the flow of things to ensure the accuracy and implementation of the plans.

I can also imagine there to be lay workers such as cooks, bakers, and water suppliers responsible for keeping the bodies of the laborers replenished and well fed. Super organized with superior minds.

These people were so of one mind and of one accord and extremely focused with one purpose and intent that they were unstoppable. There was no division, there was no envy, no strife or discord. Only the determination and the tenacious determination to succeed and to stay on the course of completion, and it was implemented were in the hearts of them all.

But it went against God's purpose and plan. The scripture unfolds in the Book of Genesis 11: 1–9 and recorded in some text to

have occurred around 2242 to 2206 BC and was a post-flood rebellion against God by Noah's descendants. It reads as follows.

Now the whole earth has one language and the same words. And as people migrated from the east, they found a plain in the land of Shinar and settled there. And they said to one another, "Come, let us make bricks, and burn them thor- oughly." And they had brick for stone, and bitumen for mortar. Then they said, "Come, let us build ourselves a city and a tower with its top in the heavens, and let us make a name for our- selves, lest we be dispersed over the face of the whole earth." (Gen. 11:1–4)

And the Lord came down to see the city and the tower, which the children of man had built. And the Lord said, "Behold, they are one people, and they have all one language, and this is only the beginning of what they will do. And nothing that they propose to do will now be impossible for them. Come, let us go down and there con- fuse their language, so that they may not under- stand one another's speech." (Gen. 11:5–7)

God recognized the capability of man, the good, the bad, and the ugly. Somewhere in Scripture it reads that nothing shall be impossible to them that believe (Mark 9:23). Jesus said unto him, "If thou canst believe, all things are possible to him that believeth."

Notice what the Almighty said, "This is only the beginning of what they will do and nothing that they propose to do will now be impossible for them."

Do we dare to believe the very words of Jesus? Do we dare to increase our faith by trusting and taking him at his words.

"For verily I say unto you, that whosoever shall say unto this mountain, Be thou removed, and be thou cast into the sea; and shall not doubt in his heart but shall believe that those things which he saith shall come to pass; he shall have whatsoever he saith" (Mark 11:23).

Those words are designed for every blood brought saint of God today. "Again I say unto you, That if two of you shall agree on earth as touching anything that they shall ask, it shall be done for them of my Father which is in heaven. For where two or three are gathered together in my name, there am I in the midst of them" (Matt. 18:19–20).

The Bible teaches that Elijah was a man just like you and me, who when he prayed that it didn't rain for three days, and the Lord heard and answered Elijah's prayer, and it didn't rain for three days (James 5:17). A flesh and blood natural man; not an angel but a man that walked and talked like you and me.

Another thing that fascinates me, and perhaps some of you, my readers too, is how great and strong God's people of old, their faith, was. It appears without all these advantages in science, plus the modern technologies our education and medicine, we have that we rely more on them and our own selves than Our God.

The progress of time has caused too many distractions in my opinion. Obviously, I believe that progress is super good because we've come a very long way since biblical time. But when I think on Old Testament accounts, there seem to have been a fair of devilment happening then as well as now.

Recalling idolatry and false gods and false prophets was a serious concern for God's people. God told the people, "Thou shalt have no other God besides me," the very first of the ten commandments!

The Ten Commandments

- You shall have no other God's before me.
- Thou shalt not make unto thee any graven images.
- Thou shalt not take the name of the Lord thy God in vain.
- Remember the Sabbath day and keep it Holy.
- Honor your father and mother.

- Thou shalt not kill.
- Thou shalt not commit adultery.
- Thou shalt not steal.

Every generation will have its challenges because after "all we are a chosen generation, a peculiar people and a royal priesthood" (1 Pe. 2:9) Remembering too that didn't their backsliding so far into sin and temptation angered God to commission Noah to build an ark? You know the story from Genesis 6:5–7.

I would be the first to admit that the comforts of my own personal life have competed with personal time to spend in my Bible study and prayer time and meditation with Jesus. I've had to be intentional about my spiritual well-being and walk with Christ Jesus my Lord. And that's what made me determined to make those things my priority. Amen.

We must be about God's business. He's looking for laborers to work in the vineyard because the harvest is plenteous but the laborers are few. If I can't be part of the solution for witnessing and recruiting souls for the kingdom's sake, then I need to check myself. Maybe I'm not causing division, but I'm not taking a stand against it for fear of man. I may not be causing strife, but I'm showing love to my brother either. God said, "I would that you were hot or cold, but if you're lukewarm I will spew you out of my mouth." By doing nothing to build the kingdom of God, then I'm part of the problem that causes division, and a house divided against itself shall not stand. Let us consider our ways and make a change.

Notes

Chapter Four

Counting the Cost

Jesus said, "Now great multitudes went with him. And he turned and said to them, 'If anyone comes to me and does not hate his father and mother, wife and children, brothers and sisters, yes, and his own life also, he cannot be my disciple. And whoever does not bear his cross and come after me cannot be my disciple.

"'For which of you, intending to build a tower, does not sit down first and count the cost, whether he has *enough* to finish *it*—lest, after he has laid the foundation, and is not able to finish, all who see *it* begin to mock him, saying, "This man began to build and was not able to finish?"

"'Or what king, going to make war against another king, does not sit down first and consider whether he is able with ten thousand to meet him who comes against him with twenty thousand? Or else, while the other is still a great way off, he sends a delegation and asks conditions of peace. So likewise, whoever of you does not forsake all that he has cannot be my disciple. So likewise, whoever of you does not forsake all that he has cannot be my disciple'" (Luke 14:25–33).

I want my spiritual family and my readers to see me as one who has walked this journey with you through thick and thin. Because I know my redeemer lives. I know too much about him to turn back. I know what I know because I experienced it firsthand.

Not what my momma told me or what my daddy told me. I don't live on their testimonies, but I live on my own testimonies. Time doesn't allow me to tell it all from these forty plus years on how he's loved on me and kept my foot from falling and keeping me healthy when the devil tried numerous attempts to take me out.

But still, I rise to tell it over and over on the mountain top that there is no greater love or power on earth than my Jesus. I've been through the fire, and I've been through the rain. I've cried and stayed awake many a night praying and fasting. We can make it. I can see by faith's eyes my expected end because Jesus did not bring me this far to leave me now. Hold on, good soldier, to his unchanging hand. Sometimes we may have our hearts broken when we see our brother or sister fall on the wayside, because it will happen. But we have got to be prepared to stand and having done all to stand. Even when it looks like we may be standing alone, but we're never alone, remember that. In fact, everyone who wants to live a godly life in

Christ Jesus will be persecuted (2 Tim. 3:12).

Read what Paul writes in 2 Tim. 4:1–18: "I charge you therefore before God and the Lord Jesus Christ, who will judge the living and the dead at his appearing and his kingdom: preach the word! Be ready in season and out of season. Convince, rebuke, exhort, with all longsuffering and teaching. For the time will come when they will not endure sound doctrine, but according to their own desires, because they have itching ears, they will heap up for themselves teachers; and they will turn their ears away from the truth and be turned aside to fables. But you be watchful in all things, endure afflictions, do the work of an evangelist, fulfill your ministry. For I am already being poured out as a drink offering, and the time of my departure is at hand.

"I have fought the good fight, I have finished the race, I have kept the faith. Finally, there is laid up for me the crown of righteousness, which the Lord, the righteous Judge, will give to me on that day, and not to me only but also to all who have loved his appearing. Be diligent to come to me quickly; for Demas has forsaken me, having loved this present world, and has departed for Thessalonica-Crescens for Galatia, Titus for Dalmatia. Only Luke is with me. Get Mark and bring him with you, for he will be useful to me for ministry.

"And Tychicus I have sent to Ephesus. Bring the cloak that I left with Carpus at Troas when you come and the books, especially the parchment. Alexander the coppersmith did me much harm. May the Lord repay him according to his works. You also must beware of him, for he has greatly resisted our words. At my first defense, no one stood with me, but all forsook me. May it not be charged against them.

"But the Lord stood with me and strengthened me, so that the message might be preached fully through me, and that all the Gentiles might hear. Also, I was delivered out of the mouth of the lion. And the Lord will deliver me from every evil work and preserve me for his heavenly kingdom. To him be glory forever and ever. Amen!"

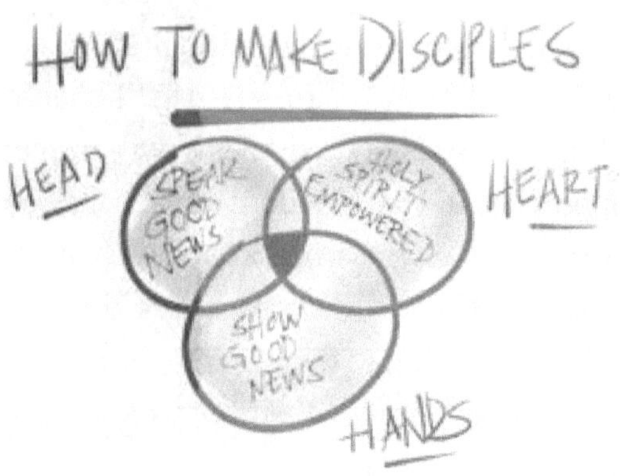

Notes

Once we understand and accept *the true* knowledge of to whom we belong then are we truly militant soldiers of Jesus Christ.

With this ring, I do thee wed!

We are in awe at how great God's love is toward mankind. Seriously, think about the condition we were in when Christ died for us. Scripture records, "While we were yet in our sins, Christ looked beyond all our sins and all our faults and saw our need for deliverance the deliverance from the bondage of sin and laid down his life for us because of the shame that it brings with it, and the aftermath and the finalization of hell and damnation that follows. Mankind was on the way to a devil's hell."

But yet, he laid down his life freely, no man took it, but he despised the shame of the cross to restore us back to him. Now because of that act of unconditional love, we have not only been restored because of that shed blood on Calvary's Hill for our soul's redemption; but now are we (the church and the body of Christ) espoused unto him as the bride of Christ?

While we're discussing spiritual warfare, I don't want us to miss that this book is also the greatest love story ever told. It's not fiction or a fairytale; it's not imaginary, but it's a supernatural tale of true, unconditional love that cannot be fathomed, only accepted and received. For the scripture tells us that greater love has no man than to lay down his life for his *friend*. Who had no fault, no blame no sin, but because and only because of love did Jesus Christ die for all of mankind.

He did not allow our evil, transgression, iniquities, or wicked behavior, not to mention unbelief or lack of faith, to overshadow his love for us and to still call us *friend*. Wow, incomprehensible and profound. Only through the Holy Ghost power that dwells within us will we be able to fathom this kind of love.

Even the heavenly host marveled at the depth God would go to restore us back unto himself. They asked, "When I consider thy heavens, the work of thy fingers, the moon, and the stars, which thou hast ordained; what is man, that thou art mindful of him? And the son of man, that thou visit him? For, thou hast made him a little lower than the angels, and hast crowned him with glory and honor. Thou madest him to have dominion over the works of thy hands; thou hast put all things under his feet (Ps. 8:3–6). And God said, "Let us make man in our image, after our likeness; and let them have dominion over the fish of the sea, and over the fowl of the air, and over the cattle, and over all the earth, and over every creeping thing that creepeth upon the earth. So God created man in his own image, in the image of God created he him; male and female created he them."

My thoughts are when King Jesus sees the work of his hands, his thoughts go back to Genesis, and he looked at all that he had made and said, "It is good, very good." Out of a heart of pure and unadulterated love, we were made in his image with an unconditional, perfect, flawless, and eternal love. Where nothing could or ever will change that kind of godly love. It's perfect, his love.

Most parents love their children and will die for them if it comes to that. The children are reflections of them from conception. We are his children and are his ambassadors that are to represent him, and we're cherished and dear to him. As a loving Father, he did just that, gave his life for his beloved children who fell from his grace to restore us back unto himself. We're the church and the bride in the kingdom of God.

So the answer to that question is *his love never fails*, and God is always and will always remember in his image were we created, and it was not just good when he created male and female, but it was very good. God desires that none should perish but that all men be saved and not perish.

He was pleased and loved the work of his hands so much, a reflection of himself, a part of himself, and from that love came the plan of salvation and the redemption from sin.

So husbands ought to love their own wives as their own bodies; he who loves his wife loves himself (Eph. 5:28–32). For no one ever hated his own flesh but nourishes and cherishes it, just as the Lord does the church. "For this reason, a man shall leave his father and mother and be joined to his wife, and the two shall become one flesh." *This is a great mystery*, but I speak concerning Christ and the church.

We are the bride of Christ, washed in his blood, redeemed, ran- som paid, and we are now not of our own, but we belong to him, one with him, by his death, burial, and resurrection. Death, no lon- ger have claim over us. "Oh, death, where is thy sting and oh, grave where is your victory" (1 Cor. 15:55).

"What shall we say to this, one might ask; shall we continue in sin, that grace may abound? God forbid" (Rom. 6:1–2).

Isaiah 1:18, which says, "Come now, and let us reason together, saith the Lord: though your sins be as scarlet, they shall be as white as snow; though they be red like crimson, they shall be as wool."

Ephesians 5:27 says, "That he might present to himself a glorious church, not having spot, or wrinkle, or any such thing; but that it should be holy and without blemish." Verse 23 says, "For the hus- band is the head of the wife, even as Christ is the head of the church: and he is the Savior of the body."

Even given the answer to that quizzical question asked by the angels, "What is man that thy art mindful of him?" It's still something that can't be sufficiently answered with a human answer that will suffice or gratify our humanity. It's beyond comprehension. It's supernatural and spiritual and infinite that lives on through all eternity.

I surrender my all and all unto the Lover and Keeper of my soul, to the Bride Groom. My answer is and always will be, "I do, I do thee wed."

Let's review the intimate and established relationship between God and the man and his wife, where the first time we see the woman addressed as a wife (Gen. 2:18–25); we can see how considerate of man's personal feeling and unselfish of a caring, loving heavenly Father that we serve.

"And they heard the voice of the Lord God walking in the garden in the cool of the day, and Adam and his wife hid themselves from the presence of the Lord God among the trees of the garden" (Gen. 3:8).

Let's meditate on that for a few seconds. The Almighty and the Sovereign One, Creator, the Alpha and the Omega, All Knowing, the I Am that I Am, communing with his creation. Wow. I wonder if they talked about the beauty of the garden or the colors of the flowers. Whatever it was or whatever they did, it was nice and enjoyable. It was harmonious! It is love. It was something to look forward to every day and to have that sought of fellowship with our creator.

1 Corinthians 13:4–7 says, "Love is patient and kind; love does not envy or boast; it is not arrogant or rude. It does not insist on its own way; it is not irritable or resentful; it does not rejoice at wrong- doing but rejoices with the truth. Love bears all things, believes all things, hopes all things, endures all things." Jesus's words were "I will never leave you nor forsake you" (Heb. 13:5).

"And if I go and prepare a place for you, I will come again, and receive you unto myself. That where I am, there ye may be also" (John 14:3).

John 15: 9 says, "As the Father loved me, I also have loved you; abide in my love." John 15: 12 says, "This is my commandment, that you love one another as I have loved you."

Romans 8:38–39 says, "For I am persuaded, that neither death, nor life, nor angels, nor principalities, nor powers, nor things present, nor things to come, nor height, nor depth, nor any other crea- ture, shall be able to separate us from the love of God, which is in Christ Jesus our Lord."

"If ye love me, keep my commandments," (John 14:15). This is how God knows that we love him in return, when we keep his commandments.

Jesus left his mighty crown and glory to bring to us redemption and salvation. When there was none righteous to pay the ransom for our sins, he clothed himself in a sinless body to pay the ultimate sacrifice in the form of a man and shed his blood as the sacrificial lamb. Now that's love, unconditional love. For without the shedding of blood, there can be no redemption for sin.

And in return, all that he asks is to love him. Matthew 22:37– 40 says, "Jesus said unto him, 'Thou shalt love the Lord thy God with all thy heart, and with all thy soul, and with all thy mind. 38 This is the first and greatest commandment. And the second is like unto it, thou shalt love thy neighbor as thyself. On these two command- ments hang all the law and the prophets. But some have not yet realized what happened on the Passion of the Christ because if we did, we would run to the alter of repentance because he came that we might have life and life more abundantly. For the wages of sin is death.'"

Through Christ Jesus, our Lord, Savior, and Redeemer, and the Sacrificial Lamb, death no longer shall rule or reign over us, and we now have eternal life through his death, burial, and resurrection power. We have to pray for the unbeliever that they receive the Good News.

"And he said to them all, if any man will come after me, let him deny himself, and take up his cross daily, and follow me" (Luke 9:23).

"And everyone that hath forsaken houses, or brethren, or sisters, or father, or mother, or wife, or children, or lands, for my name's sake, shall receive a hundredfold, and shall inherit everlasting life" (Matt. 19:29). "So likewise, whoever of you does not forsake all that he has cannot be my disciple" (Luke 14:33). "He that loveth father or mother more than me is not worthy of me: and he that loveth son or daughter more than me is not worthy of me. And he that taketh not his cross, and followeth after me, is not worthy of me" (Matthew 10:37–38).

For herein is the mystery of the marriage union between God and the Church, the bride of Christ. And the two shall be one, even as the Father and Christ Jesus, the son of God are One.

"And when one of them that sat at meat with him heard these things, he said unto him, 'Blessed is he that shall eat bread in the kingdom of God.' Then said he unto him, 'A certain man made a great supper, and bade many: and sent his servant at supper time to say to them that were bidden, come; for all things are now ready.' And they all, with one consent, began to make excuses. The first said unto him, 'I have bought a piece of ground, and I must need go and see it: I pray thee have me excused.' And another said, 'I have bought five yokes of oxen, and I go to prove them: I pray thee have me excused.'

"And another said, 'I have married a wife, and therefore I cannot come.' So that servant came and shewed his lord these things. Then the master of the house being angry said to his servant, 'Go out quickly into the streets and lanes of the city, and bring in hither the poor, and the maimed, and the halt, and the blind.'

"And the servant said, 'Lord, it is done as thou hast commanded, and yet there is room.' And the Lord said unto the servant, 'Go out into the highways and hedges, and compel them to come in, that my house may be filled. For I say unto you, that none of those men which were bidden shall taste of my supper'" (Luke 14:15–24)

There's a song from back in the day that this scripture reminds me of that gospel singers sang called "Tomorrow" that I want to share with you, which is meant to encourage you to make your decision to choose Jesus today for tomorrow is not promised to no one. (https:// youtu. be/SssJbVQOHgg Songwriters: Carvin Winans, Deborah Winans)

The will of God will not lead you, where the grace of God can't and won't keep you. The Apostle Paul had a physical affliction that he sought deliverance for and prayed to God about it, and the answer given can be applied to all situations.

"And lest I should be exalted above measure through the abundance of the revelations, there was given to me a thorn in the flesh, *the messenger of Satan to buffet me*, lest I should be exalted above measure. For this thing I besought the Lord thrice, that it might depart from me. And he said unto me, my grace is sufficient for thee:

for my strength is made perfect in weakness" (2 Cor. 12:7–9). Most gladly, therefore, will I rather glory in my infirmities, that the power of Christ may rest upon me.

Jesus knows the challenges that we will face, and let's remember that he was in all points tempted, but he sinned not, and when the time drew near for the crucifixion and what went with that the Bible tells us that Jesus prayed hard and sweat came from his pores like blood, and he said, "Nevertheless, not my will but thy will be done" (Luke 22:44 and Heb. 4:15). Jesus is faithful and committed to the relationship that we have with him, and we can overcome the world as he did.

He overcame the world and all the influences that it offered and so will we if we're led by the Holy Ghost. "These things I have spoken unto you, that in me ye might have peace. In the world ye shall have tribulation: but be of good cheer; I have overcome the world" (John 16:33 KJV).

We are all called to do the work of an evangelist.

Notes

Public Enemy Number One

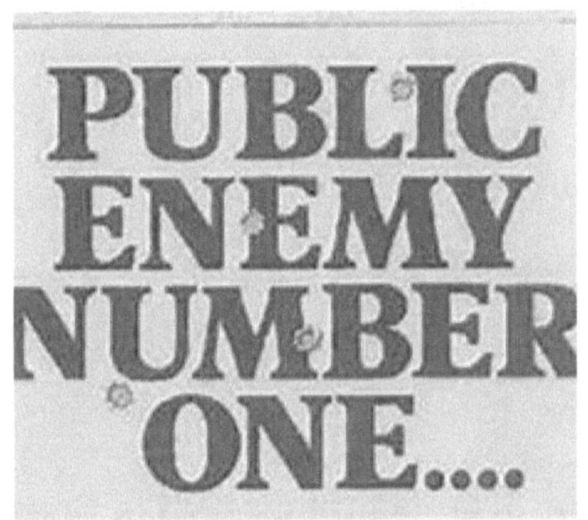

"And it was given unto him (the beast) to make war with the saints, and to overcome them: and power was given to him over all kindreds, and tongues, and nations" (Rev. 13:7)

"And there was war in heaven: Michael and his angels fought against the dragon; and the dragon fought and his angels, and prevailed not; neither was their place found any more in heaven. And the great dragon was cast out, that old serpent, called the devil, and Satan, which deceives the whole world: he was cast out into the earth, and his angels were cast out with him" (Rev. 12:7–9).

Jesus replied and said, "And he (Jesus) said unto them, 'I beheld Satan as lightning fall from heaven'" (Luke 10:18)

Name: Lucifer (Considered armed and dangerous)

Aka: Satan, Anti-Christ, Prince of the Power of the Air, Dragon, The Devil, Adversary, Infinity and Ageless

His repertoire includes:

1. Robber
2. Liar
3. Destroyer of the faith of the body of Christ
4. Serial killer
5. Impostor
6. Shapeshifter
7. False god
8. Thief

Son of man, take up a lament concerning the king of Tyre and say to him: 'This is what the Sovereign Lord says: "You were the seal of perfection, full of wisdom and perfect in beauty.

"You were in Eden, the garden of God; every precious stone adorned you: carnelian, chrysolite and emerald, topaz, onyx and jasper, lapis lazuli, turquoise and beryl. Your settings and mountings were made of gold; on the day you were created they were prepared.

"You were anointed as a guardian cherub, for so I ordained you. You were on the holy mount of God; you walked among the fiery stones.

"You were blameless in your ways from the day you were created till wickedness was found in you.

"Through your widespread trade you were filled with violence, and you sinned. So I drove you in disgrace from the mount of God, and I expelled you, guardian cherub, from among the fiery stones.

"Your heart became proud on account of your beauty, and you corrupted your wisdom because of your splendor. So I threw you to the earth; I made a spectacle of you before kings.

"By your many sins and dishonest trade you have desecrated your sanctuaries. So I made a fire come out from you, and it consumed you, and I reduced you to ashes on the ground in the sight of all who were watching.

"All the nations who knew you are appalled at you; you have come to a horrible end and will be no more." (Ezek. 28:12–19)

How you have fallen from heaven, morning star, son of the dawn! You have been cast down to the earth, you who once laid low the nations!

You said in your heart, "I will ascend to the
heavens; I will raise my throne above the stars of God;
I will sit enthroned on the mount of assem- bly, on
the utmost heights of Mount Zaphon.

"I will ascend above the tops of the clouds; I will
make myself like the Most High."

But you are brought down to the realm of the
dead, to the depths of the pit. (Is. 14:12–15)

"You were the signet of perfection, full of wisdom and perfect
in beauty" (Ezek. 28:12), and apparently this beauty of Lucifer (later
called Satan) consisted of "every precious stone was your covering"
like "sardius, topaz, and diamond, beryl, onyx, and jasper sapphire,
emerald, and carbuncle; and crafted in gold were your settings and
your engravings" (Ezek. 28:13). Picture this being! How beautiful
and original, how perfect he was, but something drastic happened
because in the beginning, "You were blameless in your ways from the
day you were created, till unrighteousness was found in you" (Ezek.
28:15–19).

And he (Jesus) said unto them, "I beheld Satan as lightning fall
from heaven. Behold, I give unto you power to tread on serpents and
scorpions, and over all the power of the enemy: and nothing shall by
any means hurt you" (Luke 10:18–20 KJV).

Put on the whole armor of God, that you may be able to stand in
the evil day and having done all to stand and be battle ready. And that
you may fight the good battle of faith. For your weapons of warfare
are not carnal but mighty through God. For Christ have prewarned
that in this world we will suffer persecution but to be of good cheer
for I have overcome the world, and I will not allow you to suffer more
than you can bear and with the temptation I will make a way of escape
for you. Praise the Lord.

"Be sober, be vigilant; because your adversary the devil, as a roaring lion, walketh about, seeking whom he may devour: Forasmuch, then as Christ hath suffered for us in the flesh, arm yourselves likewise with the same mind: for he that hath suffered in the flesh hath ceased from sin" (1 Pet. 4:1) for he who will live holy shall suffer persecution.

"But if we faint in the day of adversity our strength is weak" (Prove. 24:10), nevertheless, keep the faith and build yourselves up on your most holy faith. As the age old saying goes, "Rome wasn't built in a day." A metaphor of a great city in history, which became a rich and lustrous and a place of trade in exchange of export and import of goods. A place where they were known for building strong military alliances. All that took time, patience, wisdom, and careful strategic planning and decisions. All which established a nation and mighty force to be reckoned with over time.

So it will be with our walk of faith as Christians. But all praise and glory to our soon coming King, who forebears long with his children with an unconditional agape love. Amen.

However, let us not war and fight against each other in the body of Christ because we are now many members in his kingdom, fitly joined together in one body. For a house divided against each other cannot stand.

But a threefold cord cannot be easily broken. Let each of us walk in the Spirit of Christ that we do those things that are pleasing in his sight, by loving one another as he have loved us, died for our sins, and rose again from the dead after three days that we may have eternal life.

For we fight not against flesh and blood (humanity) but against the prince of the power of the air, our adversary the devil. Against spiritual wickedness in high places, against the rulers and against the powers of this world, which we are no longer a part of. We are in this world, but we have been pardoned and set free and called out of this world and are now joint heirs with Christ Jesus, our Redeemer, and set in heavenly places to the kingdom of the most high God. Amen.

My brothers and my sisters, my beloved, we are succumbing to the attacks of the adversary as though we are defenseless little lambs without a shepherd.

But we are overcomers and more than conquerors though the power of the Holy Ghost that lives and abides in us. He has given us the spirit of love, power, and a sound mind. And not the spirit of fear. But we are so far from the early church's example of faith with the living proofs and infallible works of the power of the Holy Ghost and with signs and wonders following. We have become as sheep gone astray without a shepherd.

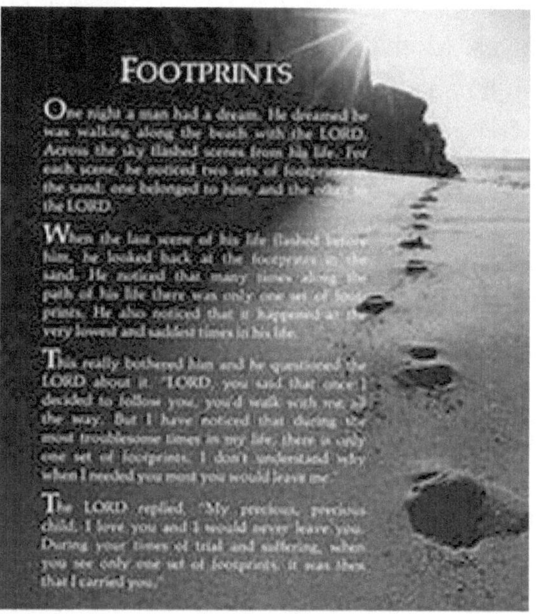

Question and Answer

Question: You might ask the question, how do we fight an invisible entity and expect to win?

Answer: First of all, unless a man first believe that Jesus is the Christ and is born again, he cannot enter the kingdom of God, born of water and spirit. Nicodemus had a problem with that. Jesus told him that which is of the flesh is flesh and cannot comprehend that which is the spirit. Nicodemus, asked, "How can a man be born when he is old? Can he enter his mother's womb a second time to be born? How can a man be born when he is old? Can he enter hismother's womb a second time to be born?" Jesus answered, "Truly, truly, I tell you, no one can enter the kingdom of God unless he is born of water and the Spirit. Flesh is born of flesh, but spirit is born of the spirit" "John 3:4–5).

Second of all, we have been endowed with the spirit of Christ who overcame the world, and now have we power in the Holy Ghost and do understand all things. If we walk in the spirit and not the flesh, I will be the first to repent and seek God's forgiveness, because we all fall short of the glory of God. He said that I would that you were hot or cold but if you are lukewarm "I will spew you out of my mouth." Church, we do not want that. It is time to repent out of a pure and sincere heart that we may receive mercy.

Question: *Why repent?*

Answer: Because without faith it is impossible to please God, the book of Revelations tells us that the fearful, and the unbeliever shall have their part in the lake of fire.

Once, we build ourselves up on our most holy faith in the Lord Jesus, then shall we know that greater is he that is in me and that we are more than conquerors through him who strengthens us.

We must be about our heavenly father's business and acknowledge our shortcomings and sins and then to study to show ourselves a workman that needed not be ashamed. A broken and a contrite heart, he will not despise.

God said of King David (1 Sam. 13:14; Acts 13:22), "A man after his own heart. The Lord has sought out a man after his own heart and appointed him ruler of his people, because you have not kept the Lord's command."
I have found David, the son of Jesse, a man after my heart, who will do all my will.

- King David's requests after committing adultery with Bathsheba, God sent the prophet Nathan to confront David with his sins.
- Cleanse me (Psalm 51:1–7).
- Restore me (Psalm 51:8–12).
- Use me (Psalm 51:13–19).
- Conclusion: This psalm shows how deep David's repen- tance was, how he cried out to God, and how much he valued the forgiveness of God.

(To the chief musician, a psalm of David, when Nathan, the prophet, came unto him after he had gone into Bathsheba.) Have mercy upon me, O God, according to thy loving kindness, according unto the multitude of thy tender mer- cies blot out my transgressions.

Wash me thoroughly from mine iniquity and cleanse me from my sin.

For I acknowledge my transgressions, and my sin is ever before me.

Against thee, thee only, have I sinned, and done this evil in thy sight: that thou mightiest be justified when thou speakest, and be clear when thou judgest.

Behold, I was shapen in iniquity; and in sin did my mother conceive me.

Behold, thou desirest truth in the inward parts: and in the hidden part thou shalt make me to know wisdom.

Purge me with hyssop, and I shall be clean: wash me, and I shall be whiter than snow.

Make me to hear joy and gladness; that the bones which thou hast broken may rejoice.

Hide thy face from my sins and blot out all mine iniquities.

Create in me a clean heart, O God; and renew a right spirit within me.

Cast me not away from thy presence; and take not thy holy spirit from me.

Restore unto me the joy of thy salvation; and uphold me with thy free spirit.

Then will I teach transgressors thy ways; and sinners shall be converted unto thee.

Deliver me from blood guiltiness, O God, thou God of my salvation: and my tongue shall sing aloud of thy righteousness.

O Lord, open thou my lips; and my mouth shall shew forth thy praise.

For thou desirest not sacrifice; else would I give it: thou delightest not in burnt offering.

The sacrifices of God are a broken spirit: a broken and a contrite heart, O God, thou wilt not despise.

Do good in thy good pleasure unto Zion: build thou the walls of Jerusalem.

Then shalt thou be pleased with the sacri- fices of righteousness, with burnt offering and whole burnt offering: then shall they offer bull- ocks upon thine altar. (Ps. 51:1–19)

He that covered his sins shall not prosper but whoso confessed and forsakes them shall have mercy. (Prov. 28: 13)

We must fear God more than man and come clean with Jesus the lover and keeper of our souls. What can man do to us? But God, on the other hand, can destroy both body and soul in hell.

David had a repentant heart of sincerity and honestly, and he loved and worshipped his God. He acknowledged his sin and confessed them before a merciful God.

I love it where King David danced and rejoiced out of his clothes with no shame. He had a personal relationship with God, and the joy of the Lord was his strength. The God of Abraham, the God of Isaac, and Jacob was his God. He established and built a per- sonal relationship with him and knew God for himself and not only because of what he was taught but what he learned from walking and talking with God. He tried him for himself and testified that God is real. Amen.

My Prayer

Father in heaven, hallow be thy name. Thy kingdom comes. Forgive me this day and cleanse me from all unrighteousness and sin. I repent and ask you to search my heart and show me the error of my ways. You alone try the reins of the hearts of men, and the most secret things of the heart are ever revealed before you. Teach me your ways and order my footsteps for wherever you lead me I will follow.

Teach me to love you with all my heart, soul, mind, and spirit and to trust in you in all my ways. You have given me of your Holy Spirit to overcome the world and to fear no evil.

Teach me how to exercise that Holy Ghost power by faith and to not doubt and to fear no man what they can do to me. Anoint me with the fire of your Spirit so that I will be hot and not lukewarm. Create in me a clean heart and renew a right spirit that whatsoever I do, I do it all to your glory and honor because you share your glory with no man and whatsoever. I do in word or deed that I do it in the power of your name, Jesus Christ, the anointed one.

Father, in your word from 2 Chronicles 7:14, it gives us the reason for our shortcomings as your people, and the reason for our destruction and why we are not overcomers or more than conquerors. And you love us so much that you give instructions for a better life and you through obedience to him. I humble myself and seek your face. I will turn from my own ways of sin and unrighteous works of iniquities. You alone are holy, and my righteousness is as filthy rags in your sight. Every knee shall bow, and every tongue shall confess that you are the one true God. Thank you, most Holy Father, for the spirit of adoption whereby I can cry out to you, Abba Father, and know that you hear me when I pray.

Now I pray thee that the words of my mouth and the meditation of my heart be pleasing and acceptable in your sight this hour. I pray my prayer be a sweet-smelling savor into your nostrils. Amen. Now it's time to put on the new man and put on the mind of Jesus Christ, mortifying the deeds of the flesh, and killing that old man sin. Why? Because a carnal mind is enmity with Christ. Amen. Walking in the newness of life because our sins are forgiven.

How many times will I be forgiven? Seventy times seven. Shall a man then to continue in sin? God forbids! That grace may abound!

Notes

Chapter Seven

A Man of War Whose Never Lost a Battle

There is one thing that I know for sure, and two I have no doubt about—I can testify that as for me and my house, we will serve the Lord. He has proven himself worthy of praise, worship, hope, and faith. I am here today after forty-three and a half years of being saved, sanctified, and filled with the Holy Ghost to tell you he's never disappointed me. I'm more than a conqueror, and I am a survivor. Through test, trials, and tribulations, he's proven himself faithful, able, capable of achieving things more than I could ever imagine or think possible and to bring all things to pass. Amen.

He is a loving and forgiving Father, who desires that none should perish but that everybody should receive the gift of eternal life. I cannot fathom how it is possible for a God who is all powerful, all knowing, all seeing, and who could save humanity from eternal hell and damnation, and while in our sins he laid down his life to offer himself as a willing sacrifice, shedding his glorious and pure blood to cleanse us whole and called us friend. For without the shedding of blood, there can be no forgiveness of sin. But because of that unconditional love, because of that agape love that looked beyond all our faults and saw our need for deliverance, restoration, and salva- tion, he paid the ransom for our sin and iniquity. Justice demanded death, but grace and mercy did that much more abound.

There is not one false god or demigod who can say as the one true God, most Holy, Jesus Christ, "That no man taketh it (his life) from me, but I lay it down freely of myself." I have power to take it up again. While we were yet in our sin, he called us friend and died and rose again after three days, with all power in his hands.

We did not even ask for mercy or forgiveness, knowing right from wrong and knowing that the righteousness of God required from us death as just penalty for sin, continued in sin, and had pleasure committing sin. But nevertheless, our Savior and our Redeemer looked beyond our faults and paid the ransom for all humanity. Whereby, we can now cry Abba Father, because we have received the spirit of adoption.

Now, therefore, there is no condemnation to us who are in Christ Jesus. We have been redeemed by the blood of the Lamb, Jesus Christ. There was no power on earth and in heaven that could hold him down. "Oh grave where is your victory and oh death where is your sting?"

"Love lifted me. Love lifted me when nothing else would help; love lifted me." It is love, for God *so loved* the world, that he gave his only begotten son, Jesus Christ, the Messiah, for a ransom for man's sin. That whosoever shall believe in him shall have everlasting life and never die. Now that is love, and love covers a multitude of sin. And this is power supreme to have power over death, power over sin, because though there was no sin in him, he took on sin to save us, and endured the cross as the sacrificial lamb, without spot or blemish.

Even the Heavenly Host and angels marvel asked, "What is man, that thy art so mindful of him? And the son of man, that thou visit him? For thou hast made him a little lower than the angels, and hast crowned him with glory and honor. Thou made him to have dominion over the works of thy hands; thou hast put all things under his feet." The Word of God tells us that "eyes have not seen, neither have entered the heart of man; the things that the Lord have prepared for us in heaven." It also tells us that this suffering here on earth can- not be compared to the glory, which shall be revealed in us. We have not yet suffered unto death, considering *The Passion of the Christ* movie, which give a possible theatrical depiction of the sufferings of Christ the Anointed One.

When I take a personal perspective on my walk with my Savior, Jesus Christ, I cannot fathom my life without him. I want to love him with all my heart, soul, mind, and strength. I want to surrender my all to him. He has been so good to me, even better to me than I have been to myself. When I consider I could have died in my sins and gone to a devil's hell numerous times for disobedience, for disobedience is as the sin of witchcraft. But he bore long with me, and his patience is beyond understanding. He despised the shame of the cross, because dying on the cross in those ancient times was as a curse; he despised that shame and for the joy that laid before him, and he endured the cross. It was a delight, not to dismiss the pain, hours of suffering on the cross, the beating and feeling abandoned by the Father for a moment because of the sin he bored for us; look- ing to the future of the fellowship that we would share together, he endured the cross for you and me.

I was only a child in vacation Bible school one Sunday at Ebenezer Baptist Church, in Alexandria, Virginia, when I first learned about salvation through Jesus Christ. I was enthralled and captivated with the lesson. When I got home that night, I laid in my bed processing what I was taught that day at church. Even at that early stage, I remember clearly as though it were yesterday saying to myself, "Oh, that was so nice of him, where did he come from, how does *he* live forever." I hungered and thirst for more of him. I did not know how to express it, but God knows the heart of man. And he that hungers and thirst for righteousness shall be filled. I was born again as a young adult; I somehow was aware of his presence since that day as a little girl.

Nothing has been able to separate me from his love, and never will be able to; it is a promise and a surety. There is nothing seen or unseen; no power on earth or in heaven can separate us from his love. Amen. He has gone to prepare a place for us that sounds like a promise keeper's statement to me. Someone with power and authority to bring it to pass. Amen. And he said, "In my Father's house, there are many mansions, if it were not so I would have told you so.

If I go, I will come again and receive you unto myself." That where I am there you shall be also. Talk about grace and mercy! Greater love has no man than to lay down his life for his friends. The love of God is second to no other.

When I think of the goodness of Jesus, my soul cries out hallelujah praise God for saving me. I was blind, but now I see. I was lost, but now I am found. I was sinking deep in sin, but love lifted me. I have certainly made my calling and election sure, for I have this confidence because of the Holy Ghost living and abiding with me. I am sealed, baptized in Jesus's name. I have taken on his death burial and resurrection (Rom. 6:3–7) in the New Birth Experience. I obeyed Acts 2:38, unless a man is born again, He cannot enter the kingdom of God and born of his Spirit he cannot see the kingdom of God (John 3:5). Have you been born again with the renewing of your mind? Do you have the Spirit of Christ Jesus living inside of you, have you made your body a temple for the Holy Spirit to abide? If so then, you are his, but if not check out the Word of God in Romans 8:9, 10, 14; if not, then you are not his. It is time to make a change. I am sure you have heard the saying, as I have, "They lived their lives to the fullest, doing it their way." She or he was a good person. Or while they are still living, I am not a bad person, I am a good person! But Jesus said, "Unless our righteousness exceeds that of the Pharisees, we cannot enter the kingdom of heaven. Amen. We must do it his way, not my will Lord, but thy will be done in my life.

Amen. We must be born again because no unclean thing share enter heaven."

Jesus is our soon-coming king, and I want to be ready when he comes. I come too far to turn around. I know that God can keep me from falling and to present me faultless before our Father in heaven, and as a man of war, there is no power on earth that can snatch me from his hands. What a mighty God we serve.

Jesus forewarned us that in this world, we would suffer persecution, but for us to be of good cheer because he overcame the world. He accomplished his mission and his purpose to redeem us and to pay the ransom for the sins of us all. What the enemy of God intended for us to spite our Creator; it could not separate us from the love of God.

For as Paul said, "So shall I, for I am persuaded."

> For I am persuaded, that neither death, nor life, nor angels, nor principalities, nor powers, nor things present, nor things to come, nor height, nor depth, nor any other creature, shall be able to separate us from the love of God, which is in Christ Jesus our Lord. Christ is undefeatable in every battle, and He will never be dethroned from glory to glory. (Rom. 8:38–39)

And because Jesus lives inside of me, I am an overcome and more than a conqueror through his Holy Ghost power. And because the battle is not mine but his, and he wins every time. Amen. I am a soldier in the army of the Lord.

When I think about myself and how far my Lord and Savior have brought me from, he have kept me from all sorts of danger, near-death incidents, sicknesses are only to name a few of my deliverances from evil and harm's way.

My own testimony gives credence to the Word of God. He

is very real, and I want to tell you that he is a man of war, whose never lost a battle. A God that will take you through the valley of the shadow of death unscathed. The warfare that we go through, let not your heart be troubled, you can trust that you will win, if you lean not to your own understanding, but wait to be led by the lover and keeper of your soul.

You will win because if God is for you, who can be against you. I am speaking from what I know to be factual. Attempts, there have been too many to even remember half of them. That I am here to speak on them is a testament to God's love, his faithfulness, his power, grace, goodness, and mercy.

God is no respecter of person, what he did for me, he will do it for you. Rather, male or female, we are all called to fight the good fight of faith, boy or girl, young or old, and we are to be helpers one to another. Amen.

For the victory to be won, there must be unity, no division, no strife; we must be together in the body of Christ Jesus our Lord. One body, but many members, fitly joined together.

There is no Jew or Gentile, but we are all brothers and sisters in the body of Christ; whereby, we cry Abba Father. We are to love one another, lift each other up, and bear one another's burdens. Scripture tells us, "Herein know we that the love of Christ is perfected in us when we love one another." Amen.

We all, I'm sure, want to hear our Lord say to us, "Well done my good and faithful servant."

The Apostle Paul said, "I've finished my course, I ran the race, and I fought a good fight." We will get tired, weary, perplexed, and persecuted for the name of Christ, for whom we are ambassadors but, we have not yet suffered unto death.

Notes

Chapter Eight

What's In a Name?

"And the evil spirit answered and said, Jesus I know, and Paul I know; but who are ye?" (Acts 19:15).

I need for us to take seriously the calling of our faith and how we walk and are read of all men (2 Cor. 3:2), how we are perceived as we take on the name of Christians, understanding that its meaning is to be Christ-like, which is the epitome of being holy. Our conversations, behavior, attitudes, and dispositions should be the expression of who he is. We are called a chosen generation, a peculiar people, and a royal priesthood. "For it is written, be ye holy; for I am Holy, thus saith the Lord" (1 Pet. 1:13).

Our life should be a light in this dark world, a light of righteousness because the Holy Ghost dwelling within us makes us his temple. We are as lively stones, have built us a spiritual house a holy priesthood, to offer up spiritual sacrifices, acceptable to God for Jesus Christ (1 Pet. 2:5, 9).

"Do you not know that your bodies are temples of the Holy Spirit, who is in you, whom you have received from God? You are not your own; you were bought at a price. Therefore, honor God with your bodies (1 Cor. 6:19–20).

Wherefore, gird up the loins of your mind, be sober, and hope to the end for the grace that is to be brought unto you at the revelation of Jesus Christ. Amen. Thus saith the Word of God. As obedient children, not fashioning yourselves according to the former lusts in your ignorance but as he which hath called is holy in all manner of conversation (1 Pet. 1:13).

Paul became a mighty man of God after his conversion. Born Saul, he said he was an Israelite, of the seed of Abraham, of the tribe of Benjamin (Rom. 11:1). But before he was converted, he bragged about his background, say in Philippians 5:4–8. He said of himself that he could go toe to toe with anyone intellectually concerning the law, though I might also have confidence in the flesh.

If any other man thinketh that he hath whereof he might trust in flesh, I more. Circumcised the eighth day of the stock of Israel, of the tribe of Benjamin, a Hebrew of the Hebrews, as touching the law, a Pharisee. And in another place, he said, "I am a man which am a Jew of Tarsus, a city in Cilicia, a citizen of no mean city. I sat at the feet of Gamaliel and taught according to the perfect manner of the law of the fathers, and was zealous toward God, as ye all are this day. And I persecuted this way unto death, binding and delivering into prisons both men and women."

As also the high priest doth bear me witness, and all the estate of the elders, from whom also I received letters unto the brethren and went to Damascus to bring them which were there bound unto Jerusalem for to be punished. He consented to the stoning of Stephen, and as for Saul, he made havoc of the entering into every house, and haling men and women committed them to prison (Acts 8:1, 3).

Concerning zeal, persecuting the church; touching the righteousness, which is in the law, blameless. But what things were gain to me, those I counted loss for Christ.

Yeah, doubtless, and I count all things but loss for the excellency of the knowledge of Christ Jesus, my Lord, for whom I have suffered the loss of all things; and do count them but dung, that I may win Christ. *Wow*, what a testimony.

However, in his position of Pharisee, he killed and persecuted the believers and follower of Christ Jesus, our Lord and Redeemer.

His reputation preceded him in the surrounding regions of Jerusalem. The name Saul became synonymous with murderer of the saints and church of God. He had himself of no small reputation. His killing spree was even sanctioned by the chief priest (Acts 9:21), and when Saul began to preach Jesus sacrificed, the son of the most High God said that many asked, "Is not this he that destroyed them which called on this name in Jerusalem and came hither for that intents that he might bring them bound unto the chief priests?"

Ananias, when God called him for assignment of divine purpose that to lay hands on Saul that he might receive his sight after he lost his sight on the road to Damascus. He was reluctant and said, "Lord, I have heard by many of this man, how much evil he hath done to thy saints at Jerusalem. And here he hath authority from the chief priests to bind all that call on thy name."

But Saul is now fasting and praying three days now, waiting for a man name Ananias to lay hands on him to receive his sight again. God tells him that it's his will that he will use for his purpose and glory in the building of his kingdom. God have shown this to him in a vision.

But it's a fascinating report of how God will use even the most unlikely people to build his kingdom. Who will believe our report? "Who hath believed our report?" (Isa. 53:1). And to whom is the arm of the Lord revealed? Acts 9 gives an account that in Jerusalem, they were all afraid of him, and rightly so, I might add.

But Barnabus, another disciple, who with Saul preached in Damascus after he was converted and witnessed how he indeed was baptized and received the Holy Spirit and preached in their synagogues Jesus, the son God, convinced the elders and leaders in Jerusalem when they didn't believe in Saul being a disciple of Jesus Christ. He convinced and persuaded them that he is. Ananias, even called in brother in verse 17 of Acts 9.

Some time have passed, and Saul is converted and in full ministry with the saints of God in Jerusalem, and in chapter 13 of the book of Acts verse 9, we are first told of Saul and Paul are one and the same (who is called Paul) name is dropped and is called Paul from then on. It would seem appropriate and reasonable for Paul to assume this name over the other now that he's in the church and born again unto righteousness. Old things pass away and now he's walking in the newness of light. Before he was Saul that religious zealot from among the Pharisees in Rome, who hated Jesus Christ, who called himself King of the Jews. He wasn't that murderer anymore, and I wouldn't want that stigma attached to him anymore either.

We are encouraged as born-again saints to come out of the world and to be transformed by the renewing of our minds. To forsake not the assembling of ourselves but one with another. How can two walk together unless they agree? It's extremely important that we fellowship with like-minded people. Who believe that God came into the world in the form of a man to deliver all who would believe in his son, Jesus the Christ, from sin, death, and a devil's hell. And what does light with darkness. We have to be separate and come out from among unbelievers and conform not to the world any longer.

We cannot be casual about our high calling in Jesus Christ by fellowshipping with children who choose to walk in darkness and who choose to deny Christ. We're taught to not allow our good to be evil spoken. Most of us heard the old cliché, "Guilt by association," or here's another one, "People will judge your character by the company that you keep." "Give no place to the devil" (Eph. 4:27).

Even the evil spirits knew who Paul was because it is written in Acts 19:11–12, "And God wrought special miracles by the hands of Paul. So that from his body were brought unto the sick handkerchiefs or aprons, and the diseases departed from them, and the evil spirits went out of them."

Matthew 8:28–32 gives one of the many times that Jesus cast out demons. "And when he (Jesus) was come to the other into the country of the Gergesenes, there met him two possessed with devils coming out of the tombs, exceeding fierce, so that no man might pass by that way. And behold, they (the possessed) cried out, saying, 'Shall have we to do with thee, Jesus, thou Son of God? Art, thou come hither to torment us before the time?'"

The demons knew who Jesus was and knew his name and spoke to him with fear and reverence. We have that same power and authority through the Holy Ghost and through his name coupled with faith and doubting nothing.

So the question is asked, "And the evil spirit answered and said, 'Jesus, I know, Paul, I know; include your name here, I know; but who are ye?" (Acts 19:13–17).

There were certain Jews during the time of Paul who were called vagabond Jews or wandering Jews called Exorcist. Not to mention sorcery was practiced openly, divination was commonplace. Acts 16:16-18

"And it came to pass, as we went to prayer, a certain damsel possessed with a spirit of divination met us, which brought her masters much gain by soothsaying and quietly as it may be today as well" Acts 16:16–18). "And many believed Paul's ministry and the name of Jesus was magnified and many believed and confessed and showed their deeds. Many of them also which used curious arts brought their books together and burned them before all men. So mightily grew the word of God and prevailed" (Acts 19:17–20).

To be battle ready, we can't hide from it or pretend that it only happened back then but not in our time. Denial is the best weapon used against us to defeat us and destroy us and the fear of the unknown.

Remember the scripture in Hosea 4:6, "My people are destroyed for lack of knowledge because thou hast rejected knowledge, I will also reject thee, that thou shalt be no priest to me, seeing thou hast forgotten the law of thy God, I will also forget thy children."

Fear brings torment and prevents the people of God from showing forth his glory and power. We must grip up our loins and pray for this kind to come by through fasting and prayer, and put on the whole armor of God that we may be able to stand against the wiles of the devil. Fear is not of God.

"Then certain of the vagabond Jews, exorcists, took upon them to call over them which had evil spirits the name of the Lord Jesus, saying, We adjure you by Jesus whom Paul preacheth. And there were seven sons of one Sceva, a Jew, and chief of the priests, which did so. And the evil spirit answered and said, Jesus I know, and Paul I know; but who are ye? And the man in whom the evil spirit was leaped on them, and overcame them, and prevailed against them, so that they fled out of that house naked and wounded. And this was known to all the Jews and Greeks also dwelling at Ephesus; and fear fell on them all, and the name of the Lord Jesus was magnified" (Acts 19:13–17).

We can see here although the sons of priest that they lacked the faith required to perform the deliverance, healing, and restoration of this soul. Leave out any other name in the equation. The power is in the name of Jesus only; it's who I know, it's who I worship, it's his blood that have cleansed me, purged me, and made me white as snow, and whereby, I can cry Abba Father, and he hears my voice and answer me because I am his and he's mine.

What is the first thing that you noticed may have been an issue for the exorcist in their attempt to exorcise the demon from the man? I believe it was this: "We adjure you by Jesus whom Paul preacheth." It was not personal; it wasn't who they preached or by their personal works from experience. We can't ride on somebody else's testimony to do the work of the ministry. So it was effective because they didn't know Jesus for themselves. Paul was validated by God himself and they weren't. That's the way I see it. They didn't have the authority of the Holy Ghost within them to deliver the demon possessed man. Which bring to my mind, "Can Satan cast out Satan?" It was like saying, "How are you going to cast me out when you're not clean yourself. How dare you?" It's a fight waiting to happen.

This thing is personal. He's my God, and I'm filled with his spirit, power, and authority. I don't need to be validated by Paul; his spirit is enough. How unfortunate, we've seen videos of huge gatherings to supposedly Apostles proclaiming to cast out devils and heal and restore the sick, and after travelling miles and spending hundreds of dollars only for people to leave the same way that they came, but worse, many lose their faith. They publicly share their disappoint- ment by exposing these false prophets.

The Word of God says that whatever we do in word of deed to do it in the name of Jesus because he have given us of his spirit the Holy Ghost, power of love, and a sound mind. And in another place, we shall lay hands on the sick, and they shall recover; we shall cast out demons. That is not what happened here. "We adjure you by Jesus whom Paul preacheth!" That is not what the Master and Savior said. In Mark 16:17–20, Jesus said, "And these signs shall follow them that believe; in my name shall they cast out devils; they shall lay hands on the sick, and they shall recover. So then after the Lord had spoken unto them, he was received up into heaven, and sat on the right hand of God, and they went forth and preached everywhere, the Lord working with them, and confirming the word with signs following." Amen.

We cannot be battle ready if we can't discern an unclean spirit from a righteous spirit. How can anyone honestly believe we're ready for warfare if we deny false prophets have crept in among us. The scripture warns against them to try the spirit by the spirit. Let's not concern ourselves with how we will be able to do that. Because the Spirit of God is truth everlasting and will lead and guide us unto all truth. When we walk in the Spirit of God, only then can we try the spirit by the spirit and discernment can be greatly appreciated and utilized. Amen.

Gifts and callings are without repentance as is clearly seen in the following scriptures. These gifts and talents more often than not are used for personal monetary profit and gain, definitely not for the church or for kingdom building. Witches, warlocks are usually from families who have passed down the craft for generations and centuries and do not honestly know any other way. This is their religion and practice it religiously. Unclean spirits mock and mimic God, statics to gain power and control the weak and feeble mind. Satan is busy building his army as well and best believe

Let's not forget that even Satan can transform himself into an angel of light (shapeshifter).

The Apostles weren't fooled by these false prophets or afraid of their retaliation when they exposed them as false. I'm reminded of Acts 16:16–40.

"And it came to pass, as we went to prayer, a certain damsel possessed with a spirit of divination met us, which brought her masters much gain by soothsaying. The same followed Paul and us, and cried, saying, 'These men are the servants of the most high God, which shew unto us the way of salvation.' And this did she many days. But Paul, being grieved, turned, and said to the spirit, I com- mand thee in the name of Jesus Christ to come out of her. And he came out at the same hour.

And when her masters saw that the hope of their gains was gone, they caught Paul and Silas, and drew them into the marketplace unto the rulers, and brought them to the magistrates, saying, 'These men, being Jews, do exceedingly trouble our city, and teach customs, which are not lawful for us to receive, neither to observe, being Romans.'

:And the multitude rose up together against them: and the magistrates rent off their clothes and commanded to beat them. And when they had laid many stripes upon them, they cast them into prison, charging the jailor to keep them safely, who, having received such a charge, thrust them into the inner prison and made their feet fast in the stocks.

They were super angry! Seems like this was a very lucrative business, and we see it today with the mega churches with the private jets and multimillion dollar homes. But how many are putting back into the community? Why aren't there more homeless shelters? Jesus warns that it is easier for a camel to go through the eye of a needle than for a rich man to enter into the kingdom of God. He said of himself, "Foxes have holes, birds have nest; but I don't even have a place to lay my head." Freely you have received freely shall we give. Amen. He told us that our gifts and talents will make room for us.

But I decided to make Jesus my choice. Some folks would rather have houses and lands, silver and gold. We needn't sell our souls for a moment of pleasure while we are joint heirs with Christ because all things ours. The earth is the Lord's and the fullness thereof. These things that the world lust after are temporal. Heaven and earth shall pass away, but the word of God is eternal.

What can a man give in exchange for his soul a man can gain the whole world and in the process lose his soul in hell that burns with fire and brimstone. The wisest recorded this in ecclesiastical, after acquiring all to the imagination, the lust of the flesh the lust of the eye and the pride of life. King Solomon said "vanity, vanity, all is vanity. Now therefore hear the conclusion of the matter. Fear God and keep his commandments. Amen.

Whose report other than King Solomon who dabbled in black magic, the occult, consulted with false gods and demons? One who gave himself to much learning to have come to the end of his life journey to leave this message for one and all "Vanity, vanity, all is vanity." Hear the conclusion of the whole matter, fear God and keep his commandments. Amen! Amen!

"And at midnight Paul and Silas prayed and sang praises unto God, and the prisoners heard them. And suddenly there was a great earthquake so that the foundations of the prison were shaken, and immediately all the doors were opened, and every one's bands were loosed. And the keeper of the prison awaking out of his sleep, and seeing the prison doors open, he drew out his sword and would have killed himself, supposing that the prisoners had been fled.

"But Paul cried with a loud voice, saying, 'Do thyself no harm for we are all here.' Then he called for a light, and sprang in, and came trembling, and fell down before Paul and Silas, and brought them out and said, 'Sirs, what must I do to be saved?'

"And they said, 'Believe on the Lord Jesus Christ, and thou shalt be saved, and thy house.' And they spoke unto him the word of the Lord, and to all that were in his house. And he took them the same hour of the night and washed their stripes and was baptized, he and all his, straightway. And when he had brought them into his house, he set meat before, and rejoiced, believing in God with all his house. "And when it was day, the magistrates sent the sergeants', saying,

'Let those men go.' And the keeper of the prison told this saying to Paul, 'The magistrates have sent to let you go, now therefore depart, and go in peace.' But Paul said unto them, 'They have beaten us openly uncondemned, being Romans, and have cast us into prison; and now do they thrust us out privily?'

"Nay verily; but let them come themselves and fetch us out. And the serjeants told these words unto the magistrates and they feared, when they heard that they were Romans. And they came and besought them, and brought them out, and desired them to depart out of the city. And they went out of the prison and entered into the house of Lydia, and when they had seen the brethren, they comforted them.

By definition, here are some descriptions. An exorcist is a person who is believed to be able to cast out or get rid of demons or evil spirits from a person, place, or object. Exorcism is a practice that is based on the authority and power of Jesus Christ, who performed exorcisms in the Gospels. Exorcism is a public and official act of the church, and exorcists are usually members of a Christian Church or individuals with special skills or gifts.

In Christianity, exorcisms are a rite used to cast out demons from individuals deemed possessed. In training exorcists, ecumenical collaboration between Christians of various traditions, such as the Roman Catholic, the Lutheran, and the Anglican denominations has occurred, as with a May 2019 exorcists' conference in Rome (Elise Harris, May 14, 2019). "Exorcists see ecumenical agenda in fighting 'voluntary possession'" (*Crux Now*, retrieved April 16, 2022).

The Eastern Churches did not establish a minor order of exorcist but simply recognized the calling of lay or ordained members of the faithful who had the appropriate spiritual gifts (Patrick Toner, *Exorcist*, The Catholic Encyclopedia) In principle, every Christian has the power to command demons and drive them out in the name of Christ (*Believe Not Every Spirit: Possession, Mysticism, & Discernment in Early Modern Catholicism*)

Yet we have seen that Johannes Nider and Heinrich Kramer found nothing wrong with the performance of exorcism by laypeople, as long as they did not usurp the clerical rite, which included some prayers only a priest could pronounce. Every Christian, Nider reminded his readers, had the power to command demons and drive them out in the name of Christ, but lay exorcists should be extremely careful not to use unknown characters and charms and should be aware that the only mode to adjure demons is the imperative and never the supplicative.

I was reared in an extremely strict household in the days when many mothers were homemakers while the fathers worked outside of the home to provide for the family. While my mother was the disciplinarian, it was my father who was the head of the family and had the final say in household decisions.

I remember as teenagers, my siblings and I were told if we got in trouble with the law to not call home; if we were big enough to break the law then we alone had to suffer the consequences. My mother was especially a proud, dignified Christian woman. My father treated her with the highest respect and honor as his wife and the mother of his five children and she did the same as his wife to her husband and the father of her children. I witnessed my father bending knees at the side of their bed many nights before bed.

We were baptized as youngsters and attended church every Sunday, and as we got older, we couldn't go to our favorite hangout on Sunday evenings if we missed church that morning. My parents were of great faith and praying and upstanding people in the church, with my father as one of the church trustees. In the community and my father was well regarded in his job.

We were taught as little children to pay our tithe and offerings and to save our money in a savings account. My mother taught the girls to be proper girls and to have self-respect. Don't go to jail and don't bring any babies home. God, marriage, work, and family were the rules in the Thomas household. Outside of those would bring disgrace to the family name. We weren't wealthy but a very hard-working and modest family and upright citizens in the local community and regarded as good people among our neighbors, and it meant everything to my parents, and the children were always kept under a watchful eye.

A good name is to be chosen over great wealth; favor is better than silver and gold. That is the Word of God. Raise up a child in the way he should go, and when he is old, he will not depart from it. Family legacy and family tradition was everything in biblical and ancient times. The Hebrews were able to trace their family lineage all the way back to Adam. Their ancestors were taught to them as babies and were proud as Abraham's children.

Today, we shy away from names that have stigmas attached to them. Names such as Judas—that name is taboo, and the only time people use it will be to denounce someone's character. Judas was a thief, he was greedy and destined to portray our Lord Jesus Christ, then riddled with shame and labeled a traitor. He committed suicide by hanging himself. His reputation will live on for eternity. Not only is he known as a betrayer but as one, for the right price, who could be brought off. No scruples at all. He betrayed our Lord with a kiss.

Now that is heartless and lowdown. A backstabber. Those who smile in your face, and as soon as your back is turned, that same person is stabbing you in the back.

So if you've ever been warned of a Judas, stay clear of them, because that person is bad news all the way around. They're wolves in sheep clothes. Judas's name in Greek means *praise* according to the *Britannic Dictionary*. Judas's surname is more probably a corruption of the Latin sicarius (*murderer* or *assassin*) than an indication of fam- ily origin, suggesting that he would have belonged to the Sicarii, the most radical Jewish group, some of whom were terrorist.

I put time and effort and thought into naming my daughter and son. Their meanings were foremost in my mind. My daughter's name is a combination of Spanish and Swahili and combined together takes on the meaning of "little queen rises on high." She didn't appreciate her name growing up, but that all changed as an adult, and now she really appreciates the significance of her name. Her brothers' names means virile. Both their names describe strength and position. I was mindful of not only how their names sounded or how popular the name was at the time but meaning and love took front and center stage in the name they would wear for the rest of their lives.

My name means "God's gracious gift"! A powerful, spiritual, and term of endearment gesture went into naming me. It wasn't until I was fully grown that I was blessed to know by divine revelation from my Lord and Savior Jesus Christ the meaning of my name. I learned the definition of my name years prior to the knowledge of why I was named with such a name.

For me, it was important to know who I am, the name I was given by my parents, and why they chose to call me such a beautiful name. In my prayers and meditation and quiet time, I'd often ask questions, "God's gracious gift to who?" I'd ask God, "Gift to whom? Whose gift?" Finally, I was given an explanation. Without going into personal and deep detail, my parents prayed and believed God would answer their prayer after a while for children.

So in time, he indeed answered their prayers to bless them with children. So I was named God's gracious gift to my parents' prayer for children. And of course, and indeed, I was baptized in church at an early age and dedicated back to God for his gracious gift. It was instilled in us as children about the love of God and to worship him. To become a Christian brings the responsibility of being Christ-like and living the life that will glorify our Savior. When we were born again according to Romans 6, we were adopted into the heavenly and spiritual realm of God as sons and daughters of our heavenly Father, whereby we cry Abba Father. In the world that we live in today, Christianity have become like a popularity thing. Just to fit in to be popular, some will say anything to become accepted. They will profess with their mouths, but their hearts are far from God. It's become a regular common word to hear adults as well as little children to us the Lord's name in vain as a curse word.

We call ourselves Christians, but the behavior is that of an unbeliever. What's in a name? In the name of Jesus Christ, there is healing, there is power, there is love, there is redemption, there is salvation, and so much more. We must hold that name sacred and hold it in fear and in reverence. Amen.

I heard a song that says, "I'm just a nobody, trying to tell somebody about Jesus." But we must decrease in our work in the minis- try that the mighty name of Jesus Christ increases. But it remains true that as Christians we have to walk the walk and talk the talk as ambassadors of Christ, a light in a dark world, giving hope to the lost. We want to leave a good name behind that will build the kingdom of God and not to tear it down. We have that Holy Ghost power to walk right and to be witnesses of Jesus Christ.

In the ministry, it's imperative that we be able to give an answer to those who ask why we believe. A personal testimony. The Acts of the Apostles in the early church are detailed in the book of Acts in the new testimony. Jesus gave instructions and endured them with Holy Ghost powers. There were also others that were not of the sheep fold of the Apostles and disciples. Jesus said, "If they're for us and not against us, let them be." He told them that he had others that were not of his fold. We must work together to avoid strife and discord among the body of Christ and learn to work together for the furtherance of the kingdom of God. Because a house divided against itself shall not stand.

As true Christians, we are commissioned to "Go into all the world and preach the gospel to all creation. Whosoever believes and is baptized will be saved but whoever does not believe will be condemned. And these signs will accompany those who believe. In my name (in the name of Jesus), they will drive out demons; they will speak in new tongues, they will pick up snake with their hands; and when they drink deadly poison, it will not hurt them at all; they will place their hands on sick people, and they will get well." Thus, saith the Lord. (Mark 16:15–18 NIV).

At the *name* of Jesus Christ, every knee shall bow and every tongue shall confess that he is Lord! King of Kings, the Alpha and Omega, the Prince of Peace, and the Everlasting Father. There is power in that name. The Lord's Prayer acknowledges that his name is to be praised by all, and there is salvation in no other name, given among men whereby we must save (Acts 4:12). After this manner, therefore, pray ye: Our Father which art in heaven, hallowed be thy name (Matt. 6:9).

What is the definition of the word *hallow*? To make holy or set apart for holy use. Some common synonyms of hallow are consecrate, dedicate, and devote. Its origins are from Old English *hālgian* (verb), *hālga* (noun), of Germanic origin related to Dutch and German *heiligen*, also to holy.

While all these words mean "to set apart for a special and often higher end," *hallow*, often differing little from dedicate or consecrate, may distinctively imply an attribution of intrinsic sanctity.

We dedicate our babies to Lord for the specific purpose of getting the Lord's blessings prayed over them and in Jesus's name. It's the knowledge of knowing by the prayer of faith and believing that God can keep and protect them from the evil one and all hurt harm and danger. We are consecrating our babies to God; we speak their names in prayer.

Keeping in mind that we are called a peculiar people, a royal priesthood and a chosen generation and are called unto a holy calling, "Be ye holy as your father in heaven is holy." Paul's life exemplified a true witness that God was with him with signs following and validating his ministry and apostleship in the body of Christ. It's our birthright through the death, burial, and resurrection—the new birth experience that we have been made clean, made whole, and restore to a newness of life; a workman that needed not be ashamed. Be ye strong in the power of his might putting on the whole armor of God having done all to stand and making our calling and election sure. will not blot out his name out of the book of life, but I will confess his name before my Father, and before his angels" (Rev. 3:5).

Notes

We've been given these gifts and callings to surrender all to Jesus our Creator for encouraging and for the deliverance of the strong- hold of the wicked. That our brothers and our sisters may know the good news and be set free from eternal hell and damnation. Amen. Oh, the blood of Jesus, oh, the blood of Jesus, oh, the blood of Jesus that makes me white as snow. Power is the Word of God that illu- minates and opens the heart and mind of the supernatural and the spiritual resonation of Romans 6. Who calls to lay any charge against God's anointed? (Rom. 8:33) Who shall lay anything to the charge of God's elect? It is God that justifies.

We can and should add our names with Paul and with Jesus as the saints of God with the same powers as our brother Paul in the body of Christ because Jesus is not the author of confusion. The Holy Ghost makes us holy as long as we're walking in the spirit and not in the flesh because a carnal mind is enmity between me, and God and he will not dwell in an unclean body. "Because the carnal mind is enmity against God, for it is not subject to the law of God, neither indeed can be. So then they that are in the flesh cannot please God (Rom. 8:7–8).

It is that sacred anointing of the Holy Ghost that abides within us that we have our moving, the fire as we offer up the sacrifices of praise and faith and the authority of his name because even the demons believe and tremble. "Thou believest that there is one God; thou doest well. The devils also believe—and tremble" (James 2:19).

"Nevertheless, do not rejoice that the spirits submit to you, but rejoice that your names are written in heaven" (Luke 10:20). "He that overcometh, the same shall be clothed in white raiment; and I

Chapter Nine

Pray Without Ceasing

The time that we now live in challenges our faith in the true and living God and in his son Jesus Christ. In 1988, the gospel singing group the Clark Sisters released from their album *Conqueror*, a surreal single titled "Computers Rule the world" but God is still in control. Thirty-six years later, now in 2024, the manifestation of that song has materialized because the computers are now ruling the world.

With the advancement of modern technology, our dependence upon him is challenged every day. There is a distraction with the cell phone; with it, we can access information at our fingertips from anywhere. Play games, Zoom conference calls, family chats. You name it, and whatever it may be, it is at your fingertips via the smart phone. It is revolutionary. It's a miniaturized computer.

We can find answers to questions with the smart phones, iPhones, and Google because we have been convinced that all our answers can be found there. It is the quickest, smartest, and easiest solution to everything.

Recently, I read an ad that was asking for volunteers to participate in a five-thousand-dollar research study where the participants had to be without their cell phones for one to two to get paid. I have seen TV programs where young adults experienced meltdowns without their phones. The phone has become nothing short of an addition, like a drug addiction.

Science and medical professions have enhanced the quality of life, and people are living longer and healthier with the advancement and research of modern medicine.

We have come a long way since the days of old. In those ancient days, without the distractions that we have today, Christians relied on God and the power of the Holy Ghost for wise council or deci- sions, guidance, and directions.

We prayed more, attended church services more often; now, there are a lot of things keeping us too busy and too distracted away from our Savior. We have become increasingly reliant on pharmaceu- tical drugs for a quick fix to cure our sicknesses, rather than prayer for healing.

When you and I pray, we are talking; I mean it, we're literally talk with God, not to God. It is a two-way conversation with our Creator. As incredible as it may sound, it is real, and it is true. It is my personal testimony. An intense and intimate fellowship with the One whom we cry Abba Father to. Amen. We have received the spirit of adoption. And now are we called children of God. He and I, over the years, have developed this deeply intense, personal, and intimate relationship that cannot be broken. It is that unconditional love, which has bound us to each other so deeply, so profoundly, that we are no longer two but one.

"For I am persuaded, that neither death nor life, nor angels, nor principalities, nor powers, nor things present, nor things to come, nor height, nor depth, nor any other creature, shall be able to sepa- rate us from the love of God, which is in Christ Jesus or Lord" (Rom. 8:38–29).

These scripture verses have become very real and lively scriptures to me. And it will be for you as well. I learned a song in the junior choir as a little girl at my childhood church that I was reminded of as a young woman. I was experiencing an extremely tough time in my young adult life, and I thought to myself, "If I can just find a church or talk with a preacher, then I can feel better."

After I had gotten married, neither myself nor my husband attended church, and we had moved quite a distance from my childhood church. So I thought there must be a church around here some where I had moved to. No sooner than the thought struck me, there appeared in view to me a church and it was open. When I had got into my car that night in hope of finding help for my troubles, and in my heart out of urgency, I knew that I would not stop until I could find the help I need.

After the consultation with the preacher, and after the conclu- sion of prayer for me, the preacher gave me words to keep near and dear in my heart, which were some of the exact lyrics to that song that I learned in junior choir as a child. He told me that the Lord Jesus walks with me, and he talks with me, and he tells me I am his own. I am so glad for that night because I understand now how it is that Jesus directs our path if our hope is always in him.

He strengthened me that night. That preacher was also there by the will of God. It was the Word of God manifested. "All things work together for good to them that love him and are called according to his purpose." And it absolutely did for me that night because I went home in peace and with the blessed assurance that Jesus is mine.

When asked by the disciples how they should pray, Jesus gave them the model prayer by which we should pray when he gave them this prayer in Matthew 6:9–13.

Recognizing that God is our heavenly
Father, and we are his children.

"But ye have received the Spirit of adoption, whereby, we cry, Abba Father" (Rom. 8:15).

"Behold, what manner of love the Father hath bestowed upon us, that we should be called the sons of God" (John 3:1)

"Wherefore come out from among them, and be ye separate, saith the Lord, and touch not the unclean thing: and I will receive you. And will be a Father unto you, and ye shall be my sons and daughters, saith the Lord Almighty" (2 Cor. 6:17–18)

"The Spirit himself bears witness with our spirit that we are children of God, and if children, then heirs—heirs of God and joint heirs with Christ, if indeed we suffer with Him, that we may also be glorified together" (Rom. 18:16–17).

His name is holy and to be revered and feared. A high priest of a royal priesthood.

"Let us, therefore, come boldly unto the throne of grace, that we may obtain mercy, and find grace to help in time of need" (Heb. 4:16) "And no man taketh this honor unto himself, but he that is called of God, as was Aaron. So also, Christ glorified not himself to be made a high priest; but he that said unto him, 'Thou art my Son, today have I begotten thee, as he saith also in another place, Thou art a priest forever after the order of Melchizedek.'" (Heb. 5:4–6).

Note that Jesus wants us to have that special intimate relation- ship with him and encourages us to come to him in Matthew 11:28–

29. "Come unto me, all ye that labour and are heavy laden, and I will give you rest. Take my yoke upon you and learn of me; for I am meek and lowly in heart: and ye shall find rest unto your souls."

Take note of John 17:1–26, the whole chapter.

Which art in heaven—God is a Spirit and those who worship him must worship him in spirit and in truth. Heaven is a spirit realm in which God abides, along with all the other host of heaven, Seraphim and Cherubim, all of whom were created by God himself. His kingdom is not of this world but in heaven. No unclean thing can live in the spirit realm and in the kingdom of God. His kingdom is eternal, infinite, and everlasting. Thy kingdom come, thy will be done on earth as it is heaven.

There's going to be a new heaven, a new earth that we are wait- ing and longing for, so we pray for God's kingdom to come that will be done on earth as in heaven. We are looking for that new earth. No more crying, no more suffering, no more death. Only holiness and righteousness. What a day of rejoicing that will be. Amen. (Rev. 21:22).

Let us confess our faults one to another. God is gracious and merciful to forgive us for our sins if we confess with a godly repen- tance. And he knows what we need before we even ask it or think it, and he will supply our needs according to his riches and mercy in Christ Jesus

He's our ever-present help in times of trouble. He will keep our feet from falling, and he will always protect us from that evil one as we watch and pray that we enter not into temptation.

Notes

Chapter Ten

Liar! Liar! Pants on Fire

Even as a child, most of us adults, have heard "Liar! Liar! Pants on fire" when referring to someone getting caught in lying. Even one the judges from a long-running court TV show have a commercial clip taunting one of the litigants (https://youtu.be/zElenmBV4LY).

"'Liar, liar—without the 'pants on fire'—has been around a long time," says Barry Popik, a linguist who specializes in slang and proverbs. As early as the 1400s, people would call each other out using the phrase, "Liar, liar, lick dish!" The idea being—according to one proverbs dictionary—that the accused will "lie as fast as a dog will lick a dish." One possibly related poem was cited in England in 1841: "Liar, liar, lick spit; turn about the candlestick. What is good for a liar? Brimstone and fire."

Or the children's classic *Pinnochio*, where Geppetto, a lonely old man who so desperately wanted a little boy that he carved one out from wood.

The little wooden boy would tell lies, but when he did, his nose would stretch out further and further from his face, and that would let Geppetto know his little boy was lying. So at the end of the story, what were we to learn from the story of *Pinocchio*?

The moral of the story is that if you are brave and truthful, and you listen to your conscience, you will find salvation. The author, Carlo Collodi's moral is that if you behave badly and do not obey adults, you will be bound, tortured, and killed, written close to the end of the nineteenth century.

"Train up a child in the way they shall go, and when they are old, they shall not depart from it" (Prov. 22:6). I enjoyed these story- book tales, and I read them to my children. Training starts at home, and most would agree with me when I say that some behaviors dis- played in school-age children are learned behaviors from the home and their environment they grew up in. Most of them have no expla- nation or understand bad behaviors, such as cuss words, cheating, racism, bullying, but only it's the only thing that they see in their small corner of the world.

The Scripture from Proverbs 6:16–19 names six things that the Lord hates, and a lying tongue is one of the six. Our enemy is not flesh and blood. We are not to fight each other because we are all in this battle together, and we need each other to stand against the real enemy, Satan the devil.

Liars will all have their part in the lake of fire. I think it's amaz- ing how easy it is and without conscience how so many people can lie. As some of us were too, but now we are "washed and sanctified and justified by the Spirit of our Lord, Jesus Christ" (1 Cor. 6:11). "And there is now not condemnation to them in Christ Jesus" (Rom. 8:1).

> Ye are of your father the devil, and the lusts of your father ye will do. He was a murderer from the beginning, and abode not in the truth, because there is no truth in him. When he spea- keth a lie, he speaketh of his own: for he is a liar, and the father of it. (John 8:44)

> Now judgment is upon this world; now the prince of this world will be cast out. Now is the time for judgment on this world; now the prince of this world will be driven out. The time for judging this world has come, when Satan, the ruler of this world, will be cast out. (John 12:31)

> Hereafter I will not talk much with you: for the
> prince of this world cometh, and hath noth- ing in
> me. (John 14:30)

A seared conscience is one that is completely dead. It is cal-loused over so that we cannot feel anything. When our conscience is seared, our lives become hypocritical.

The conscience is the God-given moral consciousness within each of us. "Speaking lies in hypocrisy; having their conscience seared with a hot iron (1 Tim. 4:1–2).

If our conscience condemns us, we know that God is greater than our conscience and that he knows everything. And so, my dear friends, if our conscience does not condemn us, we have courage in God's presence. We receive from him whatever we ask, because we obey his commands and do what pleases him.

"If our conscience condemns us, we know that God greater than our hearts, and he knows everything" (1 John 3:20–24). One of my own personal sayings that keeps me rooted in Christ is a personal quote by me to me, "I am not better than anyone else. I am just bet- ter off by the blood of the Lamb." Because the Bible says he alone is holy and that our righteousness is as filthy rags.

It is just a little white lie; it is not like anybody is going to know the truth. Everybody does it. Everybody lies. It is not like anybody is going to hell over a little white lie.

I dare to say, not everybody lies. It is better to say nothing or plead the fifth, then to jeopardize our soul salvation. I once answered a question that I refused to lie about or to incriminate myself that I answered like this, "That is on a need-to-know basis," or even, "I refuse to answer on the basis that it may incrimination myself and to allow anyone to force me into a fight or fly situation."

The fear of God and my desire for eternal life in heaven with my Father and Creator is who I chose to fear and not man. "Do not fear those who kill the body but are unable to kill the soul; but fear him who is able to destroy both soul and body in hell" (Matt. 10:28). He hates liars.

But if we have a strong spiritual conviction, and our conscience is uncertain of where it is that we stand in the kingdom of God, and if there is any question of doubt then we have a responsibility to ourselves to make "our calling and election sure" because "many are called, but few are chosen." We can go to the Father in prayer cast- ing all of cares upon, for he cares for us and because we serve not a high priest that cannot be touch by our infirmities. See 2 Peter 1:10,

Matthew 22:14, 1 Peter 5:7, and Hebrews 4:15

"Godly sorrow works repentance" (2 Cor. 7:10), and if we con- fess our sins, God is merciful and just to forgive us (1 John 1:9). God told us how to pray, and if we pray that prayer daily, it's being careful that we keep ourselves from lying and all sin. "And forgive us our debts as we forgive our debtors."

Let me share with you two biblical stories of consequences for lying. The first one is from the early Christian church found in the book of Acts 5 of a married couple by the names of Ananias and Sapphira. As is today, the early church would give of their access to the church to help the less fortunate and to show the love of Jesus's church. Today, we call this a love offering. We give of our abun- dance because we've been blessed, and so we offer up an offering of gratitude.

We don't encourage the body of Christ to neglect their own household to feed the poor, however, when we're in a good position to help the kingdom of God, in whatever manner that we can, then we should because if our cups are running over, then we should share the abundance, and then surely goodness and mercy shall follow us all the days of our lives. And is it not written that it is better to give than to receive? (Act 20: 35) Amen.

Sapphira's name means *beautiful* or *pleasant*—the same name given to that precious stone of deep purple blue, the sapphire. Ananias means "Jehovah is gracious," and God certainly had been gracious to him.

This couple were members of the early Christian church, and my guess is they were of some nobility or prestige and most notably quite wealthy. As Christians of some stature, it was expected of them to give to the church. Barnabas had sold his land and gave the proceeds to Peter and the Apostles.

In my research, I learned that Ananias was a follower of Christ Jesus in Damascus and considered a devout man according to the law. He is also noted for befriending Saul of Tarsus immediately after his conversion and conveyed Christ's commission to him. It becomes immediately apparent that Ananias was learned in both the law of Moses and the ministry of the Messiah.

I'm sure, same as today, that is quite the impression a lot of people aspire to attain. But why? What is the true and real motive for this type of aspiration? People equate much book knowledge to power. A means to power, status, and position. Remember 1 John 2: 16, "The lust of the flesh, the pride of life, the lust of the eye, comes not from the Father, but from the world. And pride goes the fall. "Pride goth before destruction and a haughty spirit before a fall" (Prov. 16:18–19).

Ananias probably felt obligated to follow suit, and Barnabas's examples, and to save face, so he also sold his land. We should be able to do things just because. We should never feel a sense of obligation in our relationship with God. First of all, what can we render unto God for the many benefits that he has shown toward us?

"What shall I render unto the Lord for all his benefits toward me? I will take the cup of salvation and call upon the name of the Lord. I will pay my vows unto the Lord now in the presence of all his people" (Ps. 116:12–17).

The Bible teaches us, "The love of money is the root of all evil." I've heard it said that everybody has a price or can be brought, but actually, it is written, "What can a man give in exchange for his soul?"

Or "What does it profit a man to gain the whole world and then to lose his very soul?" There's an old saying, "Everything that glitters is not gold." So many scriptures that warn against that spirit that lust after the flesh. Another Scripture that I think is worth mentioning is "It's easier for a camel to go through the eye of a needle than for a rich man to enter into the kingdom of God." Amen.

I don't believe that any of us can boast about what we will do or won't do in certain situations. That is why we must pray without ceasing and that we enter not into temptation because the spirit is indeed willing to do the right thing, but the flesh is weak and who can know the heart of man except God himself and the Holy Ghost that is within us that will lead and guide us unto all truth. Amen.

Let's look closer at Ananias for a second. First, his conscience didn't convict him, second, he planned beforehand with his wife Sapphira to lie about what they were going to say about the money and sealed the plan in agreement, and third, he worshipped God with his mouth, but his heart was far from God

"Will a man rob God? Yet ye have robbed me. But ye say, 'Wherein have we robbed thee?' In tithes and offerings. Ye are cursed with a curse: for ye have robbed me, even this whole nation" (Mal. 3:8-9).

Maybe, we don't fully understand that and can't compre- hend the nature of God. His ways are not our ways, neither are his thoughts our thoughts as far above heaven is from the earth. It is literally impossible to even come close to understanding the Almighty God. So let us lean not to our own understanding but acknowledge God in all our ways, and he will direct our path.

It's too dangerous, so much so, Scripture teaches that a carnal mind is enmity between men and God. We have to kill this flesh daily and then to walk in the spirit, and we won't do the things of the flesh. Amen. The spirit understands the spirit, and the flesh understands the flesh. We can't serve both; we have to separate and set apart. Jesus said to come out from among them (out of the world) and be separate because you can't serve two masters. You either love the one and hate the other. You can't serve two masters. There's an ole saying, "You can't have your cake and eat it too." But you'll always have those defiant ones who will say to that "Why not, right?" Of course! God is a jealous god, and he shares his glory with nobody. Amen.

So we can see the true nature of Ananias's character coming forth, and we should be careful to accept the revelation and discernment of the Holy Ghost, whether you like it or not. Has he not warned us "to be aware of wolves in sheep clothing. Because even the devil can adorn himself as an angel of light"? (2 Cor. 11:14).

I'm really not trying to cast shade on Ananias's character or throw him under the bus because he did play a pivotal part in Saul's (Paul) conversion; however, one must accept the revelation of a person's character and to not pre- tend or even lie to ourselves out of loy- alty for the person. But let me encour- age my readers with this  advice: when a person show themselves, believe it, please, and don't turn a blind eye at what's right in front of you. You're only doing yourself the greater damage. Have you ever heard the saying about the blind leading the blind and they fall into the ditch? Same scenario here

The Death of Herod

And Herod was highly displeased with them, of Tyre and Sidon, but they came with one accord to him, and, having made Blastus the king's chamberlain their friend, desired peace because their country was nourished by the king's *country*. And upon a set day Herod, arrayed in royal apparel, sat upon his throne, and made an oration unto them. And the people gave a shout, *saying, "It is* the voice of a god, and not of a man." And immediately the angel of the Lord smote him, because he gave not God the glory, and he was eaten of worms and gave up the ghost.

But the word of God grew and multiplied. And Barnabas and Saul returned from Jerusalem, when they had fulfilled *their* ministry, and took with them John, whose surname was Mark. (Acts 12:20–24)

Notes

Chapter Eleven

The Power and the Magnitude of the New Covenant

The New Covenant is the covenant made after the Old Covenant was done away with, with the birth of John the Baptist, who came to prepare the way for our Messiah, the way of the King, our Lord and Savior Jesus Christ. Matthew 5:10, 17–20 said, "Think not that I am come to destroy the law or the prophets I am not come to destroy but to fulfil. For verily I say unto you, till heaven and earth pass, one jot or one tittle shall in no wise pass from the law till all be fulfilled. Whosoever therefore shall break one of these least commandments, and shall teach men so, he shall be called the least in the kingdom of heaven, but whosoever shall do and teach them, the same shall be called great in the kingdom of heaven. For I say unto you, that except your righteousness shall exceed the righteousness of the scribes and Pharisees, ye shall in no case enter into the kingdom of heaven."

"For what the law could not do, in that it was weak through the flesh, God sending his own Son in the likeness of sinful flesh, and for sin, condemned sin in the flesh" (Rom. 8:3). John 1:29—Jesus the Lamb of God, Priest at the Temple of God, and the Ark of the Covenant.

The ark is to be placed under a veil to conceal.

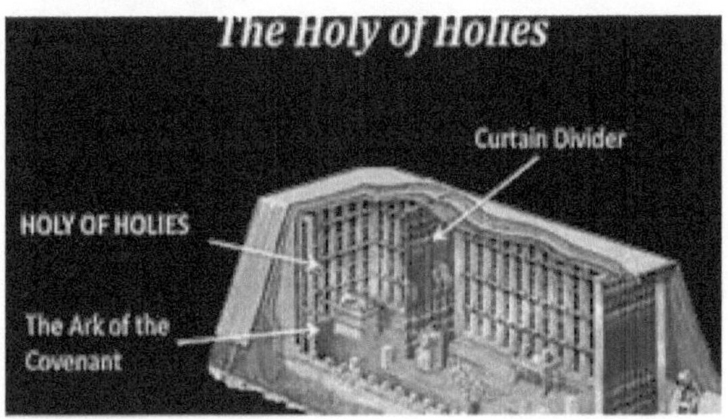

For the law having a shadow of good things to come, and not the very image of the things, can never with those sacrifices which they offered year by year continually make the comers there- unto perfect.

For then would they not have ceased to be offered? because that the worshippers once purged should have had no more conscience of sins.

But in those sacrifices, there is a remembrance again made of sins every year.

For it is not possible that the blood of bulls and of goats should take away sins.

Wherefore when he cometh into the world, he saith, Sacrifice and offering thou wouldest not, but a body hast thou prepared me:

In burnt offerings and sacrifices for sin thou hast had no pleasure.

Then said I, Lo, I come (in the volume of the book it is written of me,) to do thy will, O God.

Above when he said, Sacrifice and offering and burnt offerings and offering for sin thou wouldest not, neither hadst pleasure therein; which are offered by the law;

Then said he, Lo, I come to do thy will, O God. He taketh away the first, that he may estab- lish the second.

By the which will we are sanctified through the offering of the body of Jesus Christ once for all.

And every priest standeth daily minister- ing and offering oftentimes the same sacrifices, which can never take away sins:

But this man, after he had offered one sac- rifice for sins forever, sat down on the right hand of God;

From henceforth expecting till his enemies be

made his footstool.

For by one offering he hath perfected for- ever them that are sanctified.

Whereof the Holy Ghost also is a witness to us: for after that he had said before,

This is the covenant that I will make with them after those days, saith the Lord, I will put my laws into their hearts, and in their minds will I write them;

And their sins and iniquities will I remem- ber no more.

Now where remission of these is, there is no more offering for sin.

Having therefore, brethren, boldness to enter into the holiest by the blood of Jesus,

By a new and living way, which he hath consecrated for us, through the veil, that is to say, his flesh;

And having a high priest over the house of God;

Let us draw near with a true heart in full assurance of faith, having our hearts sprinkled from an evil conscience, and our bodies washed with pure water.

Let us hold fast the profession of our faith without wavering; (for he is faithful that promised;)

And let us consider one another to provoke unto love and to good works:

Not forsaking the assembling of ourselves together, as the manner of some is but exhorting one another: and so much the more, as ye see the day approaching.

For if we sin willfully after that we have received the knowledge of the truth, there remaineth no more sacrifice for sins,

But a certain fearful looking for of judgment and fiery indignation, which shall devour the adversaries.

He that despised Moses' law died without mercy under two or three witnesses:

Of how much sorer punishment, suppose ye, shall he be thought worthy, who hath trodden underfoot the Son of God, and hath counted the blood of the covenant, wherewith he was sanctified, an unholy thing, and hath done despite unto the Spirit of grace?

For we know him that hath said, Vengeance belongeth unto me, I will recompense, saith the Lord. And again, The Lord shall judge his people.

It is a fearful thing to fall into the hands of the living God.

But call to remembrance the former days, in which, after ye were illuminated, ye endured a great fight of afflictions.

Partly, whilst ye were made a gazing stock both by reproaches and afflictions; and partly, whilst ye became companions of them that were so used.

For ye had compassion of me in my bonds, and took joyfully the spoiling of your goods, knowing in yourselves that ye have in heaven a better and an enduring substance.

Cast not away therefore your confidence, which hath great recompence of reward.

For ye have need of patience, that, after ye have done the will of God, ye might receive the promise.

For yet a little while, and he that shall come will come, and will not tarry.

Now the just shall live by faith: but if any man draw back, my soul shall have no pleasure in him.

But we are not of them who draw back unto perdition; but of them that believe to the saving of the soul. (Hebrews 10)

Now is Christ Jesus become our chief and mediator. No more curtain of separation, and we can come boldly to the throne of grace because of the perfect satirical blood of the Lamb, which is Jesus the Messiah, the Son of God.

Notes

Chapter Twelve

What Now?

Jesus told his disciples, "If you love me, you'll keep my commandments" (John 14:15). Jesus told the multitude that all the law and prophets hang upon these two commandments that number one, "We are to love the Lord with all our hearts, minds, souls," and the second commandment is likened unto the first, "To love our neighbor as ourselves." And upon these two commandments hang all the law and prophets.

Love shows, love does, love is action. God is the epitome of the expression of true and real love. For God *so loved*. He showed that so loved in action when he despised the shame of the cross and surrendered his life as the perfect, pure, clean, and holy sacrifice for the sins of the world. Now that is love.

"Love worketh not ill to his neighbor: therefore, love is the fulfilling of the law." And love never fails, and Jesus proved that perfect love.

"Love is patient and kind; love is not jealous or boastful. It is not arrogant or rude. Love does not insist on its own way; it is not irritable or resentful" (1 Cor. 13:4–5).

These are demonstrations of the works of the Holy Spirit, and we shall know them by their fruit whether or not they be of God. Jesus said of the world, "They love me with their mouth or words, but their hearts are far from me."

"And Jesus, when he came out, saw many people and was moved with compassion toward them, because they were as sheep not having a shepherd, and he began to teach them many things" (Mark 6:34). It is any wonder that our Lord is so moved with compassion.

He loves us so much that he is calling for prayer that the Lord of the harvest send forth laborers to compel the lost to come in and be saved.

Time to go out into the highway and the hedges; and compel them to come in. We are prepared, we are armed and equipped with the full armor of God, and now the body of Christ is battle ready. Remembering that we are now endowed with the Spirit of God and with that Spirit, he has given us the spirit of love, power, and a sound mind. Knowledge is power because we have been destroyed for far too long from the lack thereof. With the knowledge that we have now obtained our faith have been increased, and we are now truly more than conquerors through Christ Jesus who strengthens us. Amen.

We are now those laborers who have been called, chosen, and commissioned to go out unto the lost, sick, wounded, bruised, blind, lay hands on the sick to be healed and to set the captives free; the harvest is plenteous and ripe for harvest for us. To whom much is given, much is required. Our purpose is no mystery, it is to spread the good news and the gospel of Jesus Christ. It is not complicated or confusing. It is not the purpose that we are to question but how best to utilize our gifts and calling in the kingdom of God.

Your gifts will make room for you. God is not the author of confusion, so relax and trust in our Savior, and all things will be made known to you for your purpose and calling.

"We have different gifts, according to the grace given to each of us. If your gift is prophesying, then prophesy in accordance with your faith" (Rom. 12:6).

The Gifts of the Holy Spirit (1 Corinthians 12:4–11)

The Word of Knowledge—This gift of the Holy Spirit is having knowledge about something that you have no ability or means of knowing based on your human intelligence.

The Word of Wisdom—This gift of the Holy Spirit works with the word of knowledge. It gives you the ability and understanding of how to apply the word of knowledge.

The Gift of Prophecy—This gift of the Holy Spirit is one that the scripture says, "To especially desire." This gift is a direct word from the Lord that is to be given to someone else to edify and build them up.

The Gift of Faith—This gift of the Holy Spirit grows as we walk with the Lord. You are saved by faith. The gift of faith is knowing full well that you cannot accomplish something on your own, but that Lord has empowered you to move into new levels to do miracles and wonders in his name.

The Gifts of Healings—There are distinct kinds of healings that the Spirit will do. Notice that the scripture says *gifts*—plural. These gifts equip you in several ways to access healing for yourself or be an anointed vessel that will heal others.

The Working of Miracles—This gift of the Holy Spirit is depicted throughout the Bible, from Moses parting the Red Sea to Jesus feeding five thousand people. God is the same yesterday, today, and forever. Therefore, he is still in the business of working miracles. Like the word of knowledge, this spiritual gift is manifested not by human efforts but by the Holy Spirit. The work is unexplainable by nature. It edifies and delivers others.

The Discerning of Spirits—This gift of the Holy Spirit equips the discerner to see evil spirits that are operating in someone's life. The Holy Spirit pulls back the curtains, exposing the evil spirits so that the person can experience a breakthrough from their bondage.

Different Kinds of Tongues—This gift of the Holy Spirit is sim- ply a supernatural ability to speak and pray in a tongue that you do not naturally know. This can be spoken forth in prayer direct to God, or in an assembly where God anoints another Believer, with the gift of interpretation, to interpret the word spoken in the native tongue of the congregation (1 Cor. 14:2, 13–14).

The Interpretation of Tongues—This gift of the Holy Spirit is to interpret the tongue that was spoken. This can either be for your- self (see 1 Cor. 14:13–14) or for the church (see 1 Cor. 14:27–28).

I want you to be aware and get an understanding to be not overzealous. Paul said in chapter 14 of 1 Corinthians, "That everything should be done decently and in order, that we do all for the glorify of the body of Church and the building of his kingdom." Let us avoid envy and jealousy and strife that no confusion be named among us. We must be about our Father's business.

Rules for Effective Ministry

The Lord now chose seventy other disciples and sent them ahead in pairs to all the towns and places he planned to visit. These were his instructions to them: "The harvest is great, but the workers are few. So, pray to the Lord who is in charge of the harvest; ask him to send more workers into his fields. Now go and remember that I am send- ing you out as lambs among wolves. Do not take any money with you, nor a traveler's bag, nor an extra pair of sandals. And do not stop to greet anyone on the road.

"Whenever you enter someone's home, first say, 'May God's peace be on this house.' If those who live there are peaceful, the blessing will stand; if they are not, the blessing will return to you. Do not move around from home to home. Stay in one place, eating and drinking what they provide. Do not hesitate to accept hospitality because those who work deserve their pay.

"If you enter a town and it welcomes you, eat whatever is set before you. Heal the sick and tell them, 'The Kingdom of God is near you now.' But if a town refuses to welcome you, go out into its streets and say, 'We wipe even the dust of your town from our feet to show that we have abandoned you to your fate. And know this—the Kingdom of God is near!' I assure you; even wicked Sodom will be better off than such a town on judgment day.

"What sorrow awaits you, Korazin and Bethsaida! For if the miracles I did in you had been done in wicked Tyre and Sidon, their peo- ple would have repented of their sins long ago, clothing themselves in burlap and throwing ashes on their heads to show their remorse. Yes, Tyre and Sidon will be better off on judgment day than you. And you people of Capernaum, will you be honored in heaven? No, you will go down to the place of the dead."

Then he said to the disciples, "Anyone who accepts your message is also accepting me. And anyone who rejects you is rejecting me. And anyone who rejects me is rejecting God, who sent me."

When the seventy disciples returned, they joyfully reported to him, "Lord, even the demons obey us when we use your name!"

"Yes," he told them, "I saw Satan fall from heaven like lightning! Look, I have given you authority over all the power of the enemy, and you can walk among snakes and scorpions and crush them. Nothing will injure you. But do not rejoice because evil spirits obey you; rejoice because your names are registered in heaven."

I have confidence and boldness, and I have made my calling and election sure, and there is no turning back. I love him with my every existence. He has been that kind of friend to me and great has his mercy and goodness been toward me.

No greater love have I ever experienced nor can there ever be for me. He walks with me, and he talks with me, and he tells me that I am his own. He has made my enemies at peace with me, and no weapon formed against me could prosper. Hallelujah. Everything that I share with you have been my personal life experience with my Savior, and he is not respectful of person, and what he has done for me, he will do for you.

We can do all things through Christ Jesus who strengthens us. I am not here to just quote scriptures that I have learned and memorized, but it is what I know and have experienced through a personal relationship with my Creator. He is so faithful, and his love is beyond understanding. He is a man's man and a ladies' man. He is that lover of the soul. I cannot say too much about him.

We must take him at his word and believe. Jesus told his disciples in Matthew 17:20, "Truly, I tell you, if you have faith as small as a mustard seed, you can say to this mountain, 'Move from here to there,' and it will move. Nothing will be impossible for you."

A man had brought his son to Jesus's disciples to be healed, but they were unsuccessful in their attempts to do so.

Jesus told his disciples that this kind comes by fasting and prayer. Mark 9:29 says, "And he (Jesus) said unto them, 'This kind can come forth by nothing, but by prayer and fasting.'" We understand the power of fasting, but when was the last time you heard about someone doing it? Jesus spoke these words to the disciples, who could not perform the work they thought they could do.

I personally have done a forty-day fast, and when I did, I journaled each day to memorialize my experience. Before I did, I asked if there was anyone at my church at that time that could advise me. Unfortunately, there was no one. At my church though, Wednesdays were our fast day. Usually it was to our personal discretion to how long we would fast. Some fasted eight hours and some fasted twelve hours and some even a full twenty-four hours. For me, I do the full day. So by the time it came time for me to do my forty days, I was accustomed to fasting.

I was so committed to the call that it was almost effortless because my spirit was willing to bring my flesh under subject to the obedience of the Holy Ghost. To God be all the glory, for the things that he has done and continues to do. Amen.

I grew up to learn a song like, "We come to far by faith, leaning on the Lord, trusting in his holy word. He never failed me yet. Oh, oh, oh, can't turn around, we have come to far by faith. It is all I know." Of course, as a child, the lyrics were not as meaningful as they are now. But they stayed in my heart for such a time as this.

I can only imagine how those disciples felt; in one word, I would venture to say *defeated*. That is not a good feeling for a man or a woman. When the father of the little boy told Jesus what happened when he brought his son to Jesus's disciple, hear what Jesus said to them in Matthew 17:17, "O faithless and perverse generation, how long shall I be with you?" Those words do not resign satisfaction with his disciples. *Wow*! Anything but pleased. Not only did he say that they were faithless, but he called them perverse as well. It was an open and public rebuke. His expectation was disappointment.

I am positive that the disciples were disappointed in themselves, as well as embarrassed and ashamed of themselves already and fearful of their master's reaction and what he would do. Whether or not they were prepared for these words, I don't know, but as far as my own reaction, I would've humbled myself before God in repentance, asking for forgiveness. I would've done what they did after that when they asked Jesus privately, in verse 19 "Then the disciples came to

Jesus and said, 'Why could we not cast it out?' So Jesus said to them, 'Because of your unbelief.'"

Remember how Peter reacted and immediately the cock crowed. "And Peter remembered the word of Jesus, which said unto him, "Before the cock crows, thou shalt deny me thrice. And he went out and wept bitterly" (Matt. 26:75).

None of us want to believe that we're incapable of doing the will of the Lord. But if you are unsure, then it would be best to follow the words of Christ in obedience, and like Peter remembered too late and went out and wept bitterly, let's *fast and pray.*

The Book of Acts tells of the seven sons of Sceva, a Jewish chief priest, in chapter 19, verses 13 to 17.

Notes

Chapter Thirteen

If I Die, Let Me Die

Whoa, such strong and deliberate words of conviction from a woman in position! Those were the words of Queen Esther of the Persian Empire, but she's more importantly a Benjamite from Jerusalem during the time that they were in exile because of their sin and disobedience to God. It was God who was behind the positioning for her purpose to spare the Jews from near disastrous and total annihilation by a devil's advocate by the name of Haman.

This devil's advocate named Haman despised Mordecai, Queen Esther's cousin, because Mordecai would not bow down to him as all the other servants in the palace did in recognition and for the acknowledgement of his high esteem in the palace to King Ahasuerus. Haman was appointed the principal minister of King Ahasuerus; and with this appointment, all the king's servants were required to bow down to Haman, but Mordechai refused to.

As with most cases, Haman's hatred of the Jewish peoples goes deeper than what meets the eye. As I like to say from time to time, when the setting calls for it, I'll say, "What's really going on?" Because as we know, if Satan is behind something, it's not just a simple matter because let's remember his intentions are to kill steal and to destroy. Allow me a little bit of time, please, to demonstrate how I visualize this scenario to have unfolded, because I've witnessed this type of high mindedness attitude in churches today. When a lay person is elevated to a position, especially in the ministry of preaching the gospel to a congregation of significant size in membership, most often than not, that elevation goes straight to the head.

And let's not forget to call them by their new title and position, because it's an unforgiveable offense to them. I've heard that with my own ears and saw with my own eyes. "It's bishop or lady minister or evangelist, how dare you call them brother or sister anymore?"

Even me, I've been asked to my face, mind you, how and when and by whom was I given my promotion in the council to which I belong. I was not one to broadcast or announce to the church and to call attention to myself, so the only way my fellow laborers in the body of Christ would catch wind of my status would be if someone read it in a church publication of some sort. It's not my intention to boast or to cause division or strife among my sisters and brothers because it's not of Christ to do so.

Somebody inevitably is going to think that it should be them and not the other person and question your qualifications, but we should trust the judgement of the board and righteous decisions of the Shepherd because the Shepherd must give an account for the care or neglect of the sheep under their authority. "Obey them that have the rule over you and submit yourselves for they watch for your souls, as they that must give account that they may do it with joy and not with grief for that is unprofitable for you" (Heb. 13:17). "And give honor to whom honor is due" (Rom. 13:7).

Something is seriously wrong when we can't esteem someone else above ourselves (Phil. 2:3–4) "Esteem others better than ourselves." We need to pray and ask our heavenly Father for help to overcome envy and jealousy because sin lieth at the door. "But if you have bitter jealousy and selfish ambition in your hearts, do not boast and be false to the truth. This is not the wisdom that comes down from above but is earthly, unspiritual, demonic. For where jealousy and selfish ambitions exist, there will be disorder and every vile practice" (James 3:14–16).

Paul in Galatians 5:19–21 ascribes witchcraft as a deed of the flesh. "Now the works of the flesh are manifest, which are these:

adultery, fornication, uncleanness, lasciviousness, idolatry, witchcraft, hatred, discord, jealousy, fits of rage, selfish ambition, dissen- sions, factions and envy, drunkenness, orgies, and the like."

Portrait of a demented woman, or the monomaniac of jealousy (also named the Hyena of La Salpêtrière) by Théodore Géricault, circa 1819 to 1822, Museum of Fine Arts of Lyon.

Envy is an emotion, which occurs when a person lacks another's quality, skill, achievement, or possession and either desires it or wishes that the other lacked it.

Aristotle defined envy as pain at the sight of another's good fortune, stirred by "those who have what we ought to have." Bertrand Russell said that envy was one of the most potent causes of unhappiness. Recent research considered the conditions under, which, it occurs, how people deal with it and whether it can inspire people to emulate those they envy.

Now it's only my guess that Hamon felt that he was better than Mordecai because the Jews, although the people of the most high

God, they were in captivity and subject to the Persians. And if in captivity, which means *enslaved*, than you do what you're told and not the other way around. If not, that person was subject to death for insubordination to a higher authority than themselves.

Haman had a deep-seated hatred for the Jewish people as they were the apple of God's eye. "For thus saith the Lord of hosts. After the glory hath he sent me unto the nations, which spoiled you for he, that toucheth you toucheth the apple of his eye" (Zech. 2:8).

I like to address myself as a child of God who is not better than those in sin and who have not yet accepted Jesus Christ as their personal Savior. I address myself as better off because of him but not better than. Amen.

But the world is warned against touching his Anointed Ones and should tread lightly because it's a terrible thing to fall into the hands of an angry God. Amen.

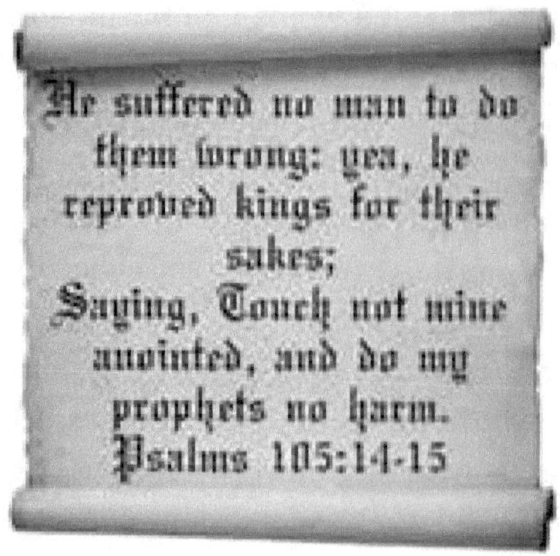

"It is a fearful thing to fall into the hands of the living God" (Heb. 10:31).

But the Bible will tell you that not all men believe and some fear not God. We must prepare ourselves for that truth when we prepare ourselves to go out into the highway and hedges to compel a lost world to be saved.

God so much as said, "Don't cast your pearls before the swine lest they render you dead" (Luke 18:4).

"And that we may be delivered from unreasonable and wicked men for all men have not faith. But the Lord is faithful, who shall establish you and keep you from evil. And we have confidence in the Lord touching you, that ye both do and will do the things which we command you. And the Lord direct your hearts into the love of God, and into the patient waiting for Christ" (Thess. 3:2–4).

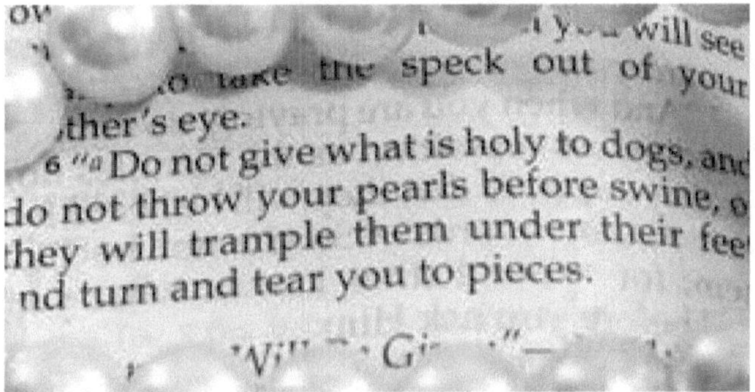

The subject for the discussion as to why Mordecai refused to bow down to Haman in such a blatant disregard is not so much as hinted in the book of Esther; but there are numerous speculations that are written by Bible scholars that are based upon the history between the Jewish people and the Amalekites and some of them very plausible too. But we don't have any facts about any of them. But what I can say about Mordecai is that he broke the law, and he did it intentionally, and not only did he put his own life in danger by doing so, but also his cousin Esther and all the Jewish people that were being held in bondage at the time in Persia.

He did not consider the consequences for his selfish actions that he'd put out a death warrant on them all. It's as though Mordecai's disobedience to the law of the land to bow down to Haman backfired, and I'm quite positive that not even he, Mordecai, was expect-

ing what was going to happen next. God knows the end from the beginning, and nothing catches him by surprise because Queen Esther was that saving grace. No weapon would be able to prosper against those who love him.

Even more was Haman's utter disbelief, total shock, and alarm as he too realized that his plans would totally be his undoing. So when Mordecai became aware of the plot to have himself and all the other Jews destroyed that he told his cousin, the queen about it. And I love this, "Who knoweth whether thou art come to the kingdom for such a time as this?" Glory, hallelujah, because if it had not been for the Lord, where would I be?

"I will look to the hills from whence cometh my help, my help cometh from the Lord who made heaven and earth" (Ps. 121:1–2). He have never ever forsaken me in my darkest hour, and what he's done for me, he'll do the same for you guaranteed. He's an on-time God. Amen. No arrow shall touch you by day nor fire shall touch you by night, because he neither sleeps nor does he slumber (Isa. 49:10). Amen.

Those who will live godly will suffer prosecution, but God will not allow us to suffer more than we can bear, but he will make a way of escape for us. We can trust him to do exactly what he said he will do.

God exposed the plot that Haman thought he's gotten away with and so cleverly kept hidden from the Jewish people in hopes of coming upon them unexpectedly and unprepared to protect themselves. He laid in wait as a fox that lies in wait as a predator for the kill.

Before long, Mordecai knew the plan of destruction for the Jewish people and told it to Queen Esther. She in turn sent out a mandate to all the Jews in the providence of the King that no one, man, woman, or cattle, were to eat or to drink for three days but to fast, consecrate, and pray to the God of Abraham, Isaac, and Jacob.

And all the Jews obeyed Queen Esther with fasting and prayer for their deliverance from the hands of the enemy for their destruction. Because if we hold our peace and let the Lord fight our battles, then victory shall be ours.

Let's not forget that vengeance is the Lord's saith the Lord. "Beloved, do not avenge yourselves but rather give place to wrath for it is written, 'Vengeance is mine, I will repay,' says the Lord" (Rom. 12:19).

We that are in the body of Christ are encouraged to be wise as serpents but gentle as doves—to be perfect in him, the Creator of all heaven and earth. If we genuinely love him, then that perfect love will cast out all fear because there is no fear in that love for Christ because we know that we are his children, and no one or nothing shall be able to pluck us from him. Perfect love cast out all fear. Nothing can separate us from the love of Christ. "Who shall separate us from the love of Christ? Shall tribulation or distress or persecution or famine or nakedness or peril or sword?" (Rom. 8:35–39).

As it is written for thy sake, we are killed all day long; we are accounted as sheep for the slaughter. In all these things, we are more than conquerors through him that loved us. For I am persuaded that neither death, nor life, nor angels, nor principalities, nor powers, nor things present, nor things to come, nor height, nor depth, nor any other creature, shall be able to separate us from the love of God, which is in Christ Jesus our Lord.

"Is not this the fast that I have chosen," saith the Almighty King of Kings, the Lord of Lords, the I am that I am, and the Prince of the peace. "Is not this the fast that I have chosen? To loosen the bands of wickedness, to undo the heavy burdens, and to let the oppressed go free, and that ye break every yoke?" (Isa. 58:6).

"Go, gather together all the Jews that are present in Shushan, and fast ye for me, and neither eat nor drink three days, night or day. I also and my maidens will fast likewise, and so will I go in unto the king, which is not according to the law, and if I perish, I perish" (Esther 4:16).

Queen Esther, at that moment became battle ready in mind, body, soul, and last but not least, her heart. Her mind was made up and her heart was fixed, and therefore, she became a fierce warrior to be reckoned with and *battle ready* and instructed her people to do likewise and to stop behaving as they were already defeated little lambs headed to the slaughter dressed up in sack cloth and ashes on the way to a funeral of their own.

I love the part where Queen Esther sent clothes to Mordecai so that he could change out of his own funeral clothes to lay before the Almighty God prostrate to make his request known, asking in prayer that he would grant their petition and to perform the Jews' request for deliverance from their enemy Haman. Before a God who is able and who specializes in warfare. For the battle is not ours, but God's.

Faith is action manifested. It was in the book of James where it's said, "Show me your faith and I'll show you my works by my faith." *Amen*. Queen Esther knew with confidence to whom she belonged and who it was that loved her. She knew him to be a man of war and one who never lost a battle and a deliverer of the children of Israel and a promise keeper and the one true God.

A God to fear and reverence and worthy of praise and worship. Therefore, did she approach his throne of mercy with that spirit of humility, reverence, and honor, as a child to her heavenly father for deliverance from the enemy of God and his children. Amen. Amen.

The Word of God teaches us that we should make our calling and election sure, and Queen Esther did just that in 2 Peter 1:10. She answered the call, and she accepted her purpose and armed herself with the whole armor of God so that she could stand. "If my people, who are called by my name, will humble themselves and pray and seek my face and turn from their wicked ways, then will I hear from heaven and hell and will forgive their sin and will heal their land" (2 Chron. 7:14). In that evil day, having done all to stand, she stood her ground against the wiles of that wicked one, the devil and Satan. Now she's battle ready, so she was destined for victory, she couldn't fail. Amen (Eph. 6:13). What a testimony that Queen Esther leaves with us blood brought Christians.

So that very gallows that Haman had built specifically to take out the Jews with became his own undoing, and not only his undoing but his sons too.

"Then said Esther, 'If it please the king, let it be granted to the Jews, which are in Shushan to do to morrow also according unto this day's decree, and let Haman's ten sons be hanged upon the gallows'" (Esther 9:13).

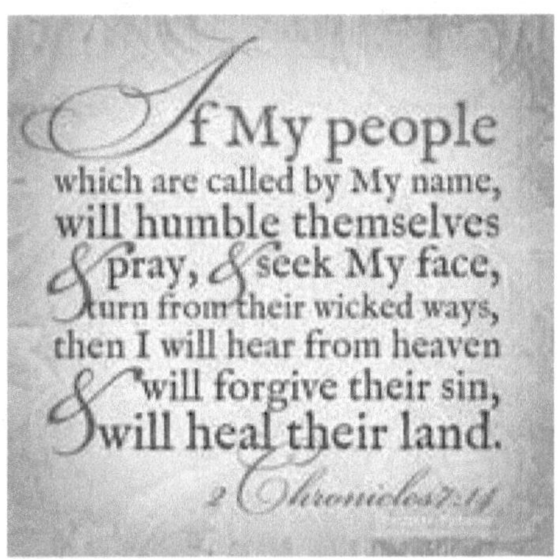

The prayers of the righteous availed much, and Esther's good works before men glorified her heavenly.

On the day that the enemies of the Jews had hoped to overpower them, the Jews themselves overpowered those who hated them. The Jews gathered together in their cities throughout all the provinces of King Ahasuerus to lay hands on those who sought their harm. And no one could withstand them, because fear of them fell upon all people. And all the officials of the provinces, the satraps, the governors, and all those doing the kings work, helped the Jews, because the fear of Mordecai fell upon them (Esther 9:1–3).

"For the weapons of our warfare are not carnal but mighty through God to the pulling down of stronghold" (2 Cor. 10:4).

Let God be true and every man a liar. We win every time. One can argue that the end certainly did justify the means. Considering the elevation in stature, honor, and recognition that Mordecai arose to. It literally blows my mind how Mordecai gained everything Haman had possessed. His wealth, position, and the protection of King Ahasuerus's guards. But it's also deep how unbeknown to Haman, he has set in motion his own demise.

We can see here how "pride go before the fall." Remember beforehand how destructive and evil jealousy and envy can be. Haman was so blind by his pure hatred for and toward Mordecai that it never entered his devilish heart that he wasn't in as much control as he thought he was. None of us are. It calls to mind the scripture Psalm 82:6–7, "I have said, Ye are gods and all of you are children of the Most High. But ye shall die like men and fall like one of the princes."

Haman listened to and followed the advice of his friends to build gallows for that foreigner and belligerent Mordecai. But they all fell by the hands of the very people that they so despised, the Jewish people.

How humiliating it had to be, as short lived as it was, the humiliation brought by his own hands, nevertheless, because to set a snare against God's people is a suicide mission.

But my takeaway thoughts and observations are that God honors faith and his benefits toward us for our faith and trust in him are immeasurable. Only God knows the end of a matter from the beginning.

Queen Esther stands out as a woman who fearlessly avenged her people by asking for the same judgement to be exacted upon her enemies as they had planned for them.

Notes

Chapter Fourteen

And the Books Were Opened

Not too long after I gave my life to Jesus Christ, my Lord, Savior, and Redeemer, a seasoned woman of God had made a statement concerning a conversation I was included in but not directed to me personally, "God is looking and *booking*."

Now I am at a better understanding of what was meant by that statement long ago but still its resounding in my heart today.

"Then I saw a great white throne and him who was seated on it. From his presence earth and sky fled away, and no place was found for them. And I saw the dead, great and small, standing before the throne, and books were opened. Then another book was opened, which is the book of life. And the dead were judged by what was written in the books, according to what they had done" (Rev. 20:11–12). *The Book of Eli* is a 2010 American post-apocalyptic neo-Western action film directed by the Hughes Brothers, written by Gary Whitta, and starring Denzel Washington, Gary Oldman, Mila Kunis, Ray Stevenson, and Jennifer Beals. The story revolves around Eli, a nomad in a post-apocalyptic world who seeks to deliver his copy of the only known of its kind a mysterious and spiritual book to a hidden location on the West Coast of the United States.

This movie has so many facets to it, entertainingly thought provoking, dramatic, violence with the most intriguing plot. A plot that shows cases on focusing to a divine calling, fulfilling one's purpose in the face of grave danger and the immanent possibility of death, yet fearlessly unaverred by the threat of losing his life to accomplish his assignment. And then passing the baton to a new disciple, who he converts his journey. He explains the gravity and importance of going the distance and never deviating from the path. How faith, hope, confidence, and trust in the divine calling placed on him was his guiding force of light.

How often he would come across distractions that were not so bad that may have required his intervention, but he would not allow it to take him off his course.

It showed how bad and evil doers were determined to use what was right from the Book of Eli to twist and to control the minds of the feeble and weak mind people and to have power over them. The mission to go to any length for power and control.

I'm not going to do a spoiler alert because I want you, my readers, to enjoy the real theme of the movie. But I will have to say that the most powerful facet that I took away from the movie is the will of God will not lead you where the grace of God cannot keep you because his grace is more than sufficient for any task we will have to undertake, and we have to pick our crosses to follow his.

Jesus doesn't call the perfect but the imperfect, the flawed, the underdogs, and the humble to do the work of the ministry. Eli was the most unlikely servant of God to be used for such a monumental task and with a disability, he accomplished a huge feat. Like David with the slingshot and rock to take down a foul mouth, blasphemous giant. This movie sends a power message of how God uses the foolish things of this world to confound the wicked.

Eli's Prayer (from the conclusion of the movie)

Dear Lord, thank you for giving me the strength
and the conviction to complete the task you entrusted
to me. Thank you for guiding me straight and true
through the many is obstacles in my path and for
keeping me resolute when all around seemed lost.
Thank you for your protec- tion and your many signs

along the way. Thank you for any good that I may
have done. I'm so sorry about the bad.

Thank you for the friend I made. Please watch
over her as you watched over me. Thank you for
finally allowing me to rest. I'm so very tired, but I
go now to my rest at peace, knowing that I have done
right with my time on this earth. I fought the good
fight, I finished the race, I kept the faith.

I love the book of Psalms 40, especially the verse that mentions
the volume of the book in verse 7. Psalms 40 verse 7 said, "I, lo, I
come, in the volume of the book, it is written of me. I delight to do
thy will. Oh my God, thy law is within my heart. I have preached in
the great congregation, lo, I have not refrained my lips, O Lord, thou
knoweth; I have not hidden thy righteousness within my heart. I
have declared thy faithfulness and thy salvation. I have not concealed
thy loving kindness and thy truth from the great congregation. then
he goes on, I too pray, withhold not thy tender mercies from me, O
Lord; let thy loving kindness and thy truth continually preserve me.
"For innumerable evils have compassed me about, my iniquities have
taken hold upon me so that I am not able to look up, they are more
than the hairs of my head, therefore, my heart failed me. Be pleased,
oh, Lord, to deliver me. O Lord, make haste to help me. Let them be
ashamed and confounded together that seek out my soul to destroy it.
"Let them be driven backward and put to shame that wish me
evil. Let them be desolate for reward of their shame that say unto me,
ha, ha. Let all that seek thee rejoice and be glad in thee such as love
thou salvation say continually the Lord is magnified. But I am poor
and needy, yet the Lord thinketh upon me, thou art my help and my
deliverer; make no tarrying, oh, Lord, my God. Amen."

Notes

Chapter Fifteen

Yield Not to Temptation

I cannot count the times that I ignored that sweet soft voice whispering to my soul's mind. I didn't have to wonder or guess about whether or not it was me talking to myself. I knew it was the Holy Ghost because it was a two-way conversation like two ordinary people's conversation.

I was a relatively new saint in a Pentecostal Church when I thought that everybody there was real, and not only was I new at this church, but I was extremely naïve to certain behaviors that I probably would be one of those that the wolves would say about. "Here comes another catch."

That devil's advocate had come to find out how long of a list of the weak and silly and simple minded and the unawares could be generated this time around? And even to this day, it continues to walk in the path of the wicked.

I was so gullible and so convinced by the deception of my own eyes that when the Holy Spirit told me not to believe or to have any dealings with this snake that I actually verbally said, "Or no not that individual." And that's when the Holy Ghost said to me after I had quenched the Spirit, "Okay, you go ahead and find out for yourself and you will see."

But not for a moment, or for an hour or for a day, did he ever leave me or forsake me, and he was my ever-present help in the time of trouble.

And guess what? I truly am sorrowful, and with much regret, did as untold, as others had before me, turned a deaf ear to the Holy Spirit. And the errors of my ways caught up with me. What hurts though the most is I wasn't hearing from church gossip but straight from the Master who tried the reins of the heart, who see every secret thing, and nothing is hidden from him.

"If I ascend up into heaven, thou art there; if I make my bed in hell, behold, thou art there" (Ps. 139:8). He beholds everything. The good and the bad and the ugly.

I am more discerning now and thank God for his longsuffering toward me and his unconditional love to us all. He bore long with this sister (speaking of myself). His goodness and his mercy have followed me all the days of my life.

I love this testimony song, "I don't know why Jesus loves me. I don't know why he cares or why he sacrificed his life for me. Oh, so glad that he did. Amen. I don't know why Jesus loved me. I don't know why he cares."

> I Don't Know Why Jesus Loves Me
> By Andraé Crouch
>
> I don't know why he sacrificed his life
> Oh, but I'm glad, so glad he did
> He left his mighty throne in glory
> To bring to us redemption's story
> Then he died but he rose again Oh,
> but I'm glad, so glad he did
>
> He left his might
> Oh, but I'm glad, I'm glad he did.
> So glad he did
> I'm glad he did
> Where would I be if Jesus didn't love me?
> Where would I be if Jesus didn't care?
> Where would I be if He hadn't sacrificed His life
> Oh, but I'm glad, so glad he did
>
> I don't know why Jesus loved me

(oh, I don't know why)
I don't know why he cared (oh, I don't know why)
I don't know why he sacrificed his life
Oh, but I'm glad (so glad), so glad he did
Oh, but I'm glad (so glad), so glad He did

It should've been me, it could've been me, but God. Amen and Amen. Were it not for his goodness or his mercy, where would I be. I repented to my Lord, he showed me mercy and forgiveness, that I died not in the sin of omission. Praise God!

I would compare myself to my Brother Jonah, whose gone many years now. What a legacy! And there are some similarities in his story where I can see myself.

First, Jonah, those people don't deserve your message for salvation because they're evil. They worship devils, and they're cannibals.

But God saw something that Jonah would never nor could he ever and that's what makes him God, when you're all knowing and us the creatures of his making. He only knows the true heart of a man.

I can hear my brother, Jonah, "Ah, what, where did you want me to go, Nineveh, that heathenized nation? I don't think so, I am not the one, Jesus, please send somebody else, why me, when you know how I despise these people. You must send someone else. Anybody, just not me."

Can anybody, can somebody, tell me who can win in a battle, with all their illustrious array of splendor and of untold numbers of soldiers and grand weapons of warfare to fight against one man of war? How can a creature ever measure up to the one and truly Mighty God, the Creator. Angels bow before him; heaven and earth adore him. What a mighty God we serve.

So with all of that said tell me who's going to come out on the winning every time?

Second, me. No, Jesus! You're wrong. In my mind, I'm going

over and over my mind all the positive things that I've witnessed or observed church services, testimony services and all. How could that be, I just don't see it. Only good interestingly so. We can't jest with the all-knowing especially when it comes to the potential loss of a soul.

As the Scripture gives its readers a glimpse of Jonah's peril—how he was swallowed up the belly of whale trying to run and hide from God after trying to face off with him. For the hallowing hellish three days and three nights there Jonah came to his senses that it's useless, it's silly of us, to actually think that we can come to blows with he who have made us and not we ourselves.

Though the consequences for my actions and behavior were justifiable, were trying, firm, long, and tedious and actually painful, I am truly thankful for the experience. I am who I am today, a holy and righteous woman in Christ Jesus able to discern both the holy from the unholy. Amen.

There was a song that I learned in the junior choir back in the day, "Yield not to temptation, for yielding is sin. Each victory will help you, comfort, strengthen, and keep you.

"He's willing to help you. He will carry you through. Just ask the Savior to help you, he will carry you through."

That song brought me to a story in Scripture about how vitally important it is to follow the commandments of God word for word, or detail to detail, or suffer the dire consequences that could befall any of who disobey.

In 1 Kings 13:11–32, there was man in ancient Bible history described as a man of God, *a prophet*. Let me say this first before I get into the story. It's not up to us to question God's instruction or commandments or change the letters of the instructions or explain to suit any given situation or circumstances. Amen.

Glory to God. Because he knows the end of any situation from the beginning. Therefore, it's always better to believe God and let every man be a liar. We're not to lean to our own understanding but to acknowledge him in all matters, and he will direct our path. Amen. We won't go wrong.

So, the man of God, from Judah, is given instruction to deliver to the Israelite's to King Jeroboam in 1 Kings 13:1–3. He did what and said what thus saith the Lord, in obedience did this man of God. He completed his assignment appointed unto him.

Now, before I go any further, I have to share this with my readers because we should receive the Word of God as our admonition and instruction for living a victorious life.

When I first read the report of this man of God, I was astonished and baffled at the same time. I wondered how it was possible that on one hand we can obey the word of God and on the other disobey. I was questioning the man of God, "Like, how could you let this happen to you? You knew God's voice because you went out to accomplish your mission with the fear of the Lord leading and you were successful."

But then I had to caution myself unless I fall into the same situation unawares. "Brethren, if a man be overtaken in a fault, ye which are spiritual, restore such a one in the spirit of meekness; considering thyself, lest thou also be tempted" (Gal. 6:1). What makes me think that the same thing couldn't happen to me?

"Because evil is always present. I find then a law, that, when I would do good, evil is present with me. For I delight in the law of God after the inward man, but I see another law in my members, warring against the law of my mind and bringing me into captivity to the law of sin which is in my members. O wretched man that I am! Who shall deliver me from the body of this death?" (Rom. 7:21).

Because when we would do good, evil is always present, and that old devil indeed goes to and from, seeking whom he may devour. We must always be sober and vigilant with this in mind.

Not to say that we won't make mistakes because we know that we're in all probability will make plenty. But when Jesus was asked how many times we should forgive our brethren, he said seventy times seven, explaining there is no limit, showing us himself and his unlimited mercy and forgiveness. That's love unconditional.

"The flesh wars against the Spirit" (Gal. 5:17). One thing is for sure; pride goes before the fall. Neither should we think more highly of ourselves than we should. Amen to that. If we can be truly honest with ourselves, we've all been there in some form or another.

> Now there dwelt an old prophet in Bethel, and his sons came and told him all the works that the man of God had done that day in Bethel, the words which he had spoken unto the king, them they told also to their father.

> And their father said unto them, "What way went he?" For his sons had seen what way the man of God went, which came from Judah.

> And he said unto his sons, "Saddle me the ass." So they saddled him the ass, and he rode thereon,

> And went after the man of God and found him sitting under an oak, and he said unto him, "Art thou the man of God that camest from Judah?" And he said, "I am."

> Then he said unto him, "Come home with me and eat bread."

> And he said, "I may not return with thee, nor go in with thee, neither will I eat bread nor drink water with thee in this place."

> For it was said to me by the word of the Lord,

thou shalt eat no bread nor drink water there, nor turn again to go by the way that thou camest.

He said unto him, "I am a prophet also   as thou art; and an angel spoke unto me by the word of the Lord, saying, bring him back with thee into thine house, that he may eat bread and drink water. But he lied unto him."

So he went back with him and did eat bread in his house and drank water.

And it came to pass, as they sat at the table, that the word of the Lord came unto the prophet that brought him back.

And he cried unto the man of God that came from Judah, saying, thus saith the Lord, forasmuch as thou hast disobeyed the mouth of the Lord, and hast not kept the commandment which the Lord thy God commanded thee.

But camest back and hast eaten bread and drunk water in the place, of the which the Lord did say to thee, "Eat no bread, and drink no water; thy carcass shall not come unto the sepul- cher of thy fathers."

And it came to pass, after he had eaten bread, and after he had drunk, that he saddled for him the ass, to wit, for the prophet whom he had brought back.

And when he was gone, a lion met him by the way, and slew him; and his carcass was cast in the way, and the ass stood by it, the lion also stood by the carcass.

And behold, men passed by and saw the carcass cast in the way, and the lion standing by the carcass, and they came and told it in the city where the old prophet dwelt.

Here is where this scripture come in, "Let God be true and every man a liar" (Rom. 3:4). "But even though we, or an angel from heaven, should preach to you any gospel other than that which we preached to you, let him be cursed" (Gal. 1: 8).

What just happened here? Evidently this man of God is at first obedient to the word of God, and God used him to prophesy what "thus saith the Lord" to the King of Israel.

According to 1 Kings, while Jeroboam was engaged in offering incense at Bethel, a "man of God" warned him that "a son named Josiah will be born to the house of David."

Attempting to arrest the prophet for his bold words of defiance, Jeroboam's hand was "dried up," and the altar before which he stood was rent asunder. At the entreaty of the man of God, his hand was restored to him again, but the miracle made no abiding impression on him.

Jeroboam offered hospitality to the man of God, but this was declined, not out of contempt but in obedience to the command of God. The prophecy is fulfilled in 2 Kings.

The way the story reads is it attracted the attention of not only the king but also other countrymen as well because the Word was delivered by him with the fear of God to King Jeroboam because of idolatry, and the king's wicked and sinful acts, and it was seen and heard by the sons of an old prophet.

So the man of God refused the King's invitation, out of obedience to his God, but accepted the old prophet's invitation? But why? Could it have been because he felt some kind of comradery with the older prophet because he said he was a prophet also just like the man of God, or was it that he said an angel from God who spoke on behalf of the Lord. He was adamant about doing what saith the Lord and determined to stand his ground as we read 1 Kings 13.

And the man of God said unto the king, and boldly I might add, "If thou wilt give me half thine house, I will not go in with thee, neither will I eat bread nor drink water in this place."

I don't believe this man of God was so easily deceived into believing a lie. Yet at the end of the story, he was indeed enticed, seduced, and persuaded by the tempter, the devil's advocate! This was a false prophet and a lying prophet, and he was of the devil. "Ye are of your father the devil, and the lusts of your father ye will do. He was a murderer from the beginning, and abode not in the truth, because there is no truth in him. When he speaketh a lie, he speaketh of his own for he is a liar, and the father of it" (John 8:44).

Jesus told the religious leader, the scribes, and the Pharisees that they were of their father, Satan, the devil.

"Ye do the deeds of your father. Then said they to him, we be not born of fornication; we have one Father, even God. Jesus said unto them, 'If God were your Father, ye would love me, for I proceeded forth and came from God; neither came I of myself, but he sent me.'

"Why do ye not understand my speech? even because ye cannot hear my word.

"Ye are of your father the devil, and the lusts of your father ye will do. He was a murderer from the beginning, and abode not in the truth, because there is no truth in him. When he speaketh a lie, he speaketh of his own, for he is a liar, and the father of it" (John 8:41–44).

They portrayed themselves as servants of God, and this is they who Jesus will say to "Depart from me ye workers of iniquities, I never knew you. Having a form of godliness but denying the power thereof" (1 Kings 13:18).

But he lied unto him. He was his father, the devil, and the truth wasn't in him. But why? Why did he lie to this man of God? Why does anybody lie, what was the purpose, it's anybody's guess. But I noticed that the false prophet was careful not to say that it was God. Looking back at the Garden of Eden (Genesis 3) after God asked her what she had done, her response was quite telling because she answered and said, "And the Lord God said to the woman, 'What *is* this you have done?' The woman said, 'The serpent deceived me, and I ate.'"

I'm inclined to believe that the man of God was beguiled just as Eve was beguiled all those years before. I recently read a little quote, "The devil doesn't sleep, he waits," which is more reason to not yield unto temptation for yielding is sin; just ask the Savior to help you, comfort, strengthen, and keep you because he's willing to help you, and he will carry you through.

Look at how devious the enemy is. Now the serpent was more cunning than any beast of the field, which the Lord God had made. And he said to the woman, "Has God indeed said, 'You shall not eat of every tree of the garden?' So when the woman saw that the tree *was* good for food, that it *was* pleasant to the eyes, and a tree desirable to make *one* wise, she took of its fruit and ate. She also gave it to her husband with her, and he ate."

He appealed to all her senses. The five senses traditionally ascribed to humans are vision, hearing, taste, smell, and touch. A sixth sense could be proprioception, the perception of body position, which is important for balance and agility in movement. It could also include perception of stimuli from within the body, such as pain, hunger, or thirst.

The bible warns of the sins of the flesh; the lust of the flesh, the lust of the eye, and the pride of life. "For all that is in the world, the lust of the flesh, and the lust of the eyes, and the pride of life, is not of the Father, but is of the world" (1 John 2:16). The enemy still uses those same tactics today because they appeal to the flesh, and it still gets people caught up in vanity. Remember how King Solomon summed it up so well, "Vanity, vanity all is vanity." Hear the conclusion of the matter, fear God, and keep his commandments. An age ole saying goes, "Everything that glitters is not gold." Believe that!

By the same methods that the devil used to cause the fall of man in the beginning is exactly what happened to the man of God in 1 Kings 13:11–25. I believe that the false prophet (the devil's advocate), knowing now who he belonged to, the devil being his father, that his approach had to be above the normal average craftiness because the truth was laced with lies to entice the weakness of the flesh the man of God was hungry. Remember how Satan waited for Jesus to end his forty-day fast to appeal to Jesus's humanity because he was hungry.

Surely, he was weak physically and famished after forty days of fasting and needed food to replenish his strength, and the enemy would use what he *thought* would be a moment of weakness to his advantage (Matt. 4:1–11). Nevertheless, let the weak say they are strong because greater is he that is in us than he that is in the world. And nothing seen or unseen can separate us from the love of God—no power, nor principalities, not even death will be able to come between our God and us. Amen.

At that time Jesus was led by the Spirit into the desert to be tempted by the devil. He fasted for forty days and forty nights and afterward was hungry. The tempter approached and said to him, "If you are the Son of God, command that these stones become loaves of bread." But Jesus resisted the devil so that he fled. "Submit yourselves therefore to God. Resist the devil, and he will flee from you" (James 4:7).

Jesus denied his flesh and was strong in the Spirit, so must we be strong in the Lord and in the power of his might. Amen. Using the Word of God as our weapon of warfare, which is the Sword of the Spirit to resist the devil. We must mortify the deeds of the flesh, looking to Jesus, the author and finisher of our faith, and looking to the hills from whence cometh our help; our help cometh from the

Lord who made heaven and earth.

With every temptation of the enemy that he presented to our Lord, it was resisted with and by the power of the Sword of the Spirit, the Word of God. What can we learn and take away from this horrible and tragic incident between the old prophet and the man of God? This can be a strong admonition for the church and the saints of God; when confused or in doubt, remember that God wants to help us and is willing and able to deliver us from all evil. So all we need to do is to look to the hills from whence cometh our help. He's our strong tower and refuge, and he will hide us in the shadow of his wings.

"Would to God ye could bear with me a little in my folly and indeed bear with me. For I am jealous over you with godly jealousy. For I have espoused you to one husband that I may present you as a chaste virgin to Christ. But I fear, lest by any means, as the serpent beguiled Eve through his subtilty, so your minds should be corrupted from the simplicity that is in Christ. For if he that cometh preacheth another Jesus, whom we have not preached, or if ye receive another spirit, which ye have not received, or another gospel, which ye have not accepted, ye might well bear with him.

"For I suppose I was not a whit behind the very chief apostles. But though I be rude in speech, yet not in knowledge; but we have been thoroughly made manifest among you in all things. Have I committed an offence in abasing myself that ye might be exalted, because I have preached to you the gospel of God freely? I robbed other churches, taking wages of them, to do you service. And when I was present with you, and wanted, I was chargeable to no man: for that which was lacking to me the brethren which came from Macedonia supplied: and in all things I have kept myself from being burdensome unto you, and so will I keep myself.

"As the truth of Christ is in me, no man shall stop me of this boasting in the regions of Achaia. Wherefore? because I love you not? God knoweth. But what I do, that I will do, that I may cut off occasion from them which desire occasion; that wherein they glory, they may be found even as we. For such are false apostles, deceitful workers, transforming themselves into the apostles of Christ. And no marvel; for Satan himself is transformed into an angel of light. Therefore, it is no great thing if his ministers also be transformed as the ministers of righteousness; whose end shall be according to their works" (2 Cor. 11:1–15).

Pray! Pray! Pray! And pray some more. I don't pretend to understand or have an answer for why the man of God didn't step back and pray and ask for guidance from his God, especially after coming from a victorious victory in delivering the Word of God to King Jeroboam in Bethel. He heard the voice of God and in acting after the unction of God delivered in obedience what thus saith the Lord God Almighty. God is not the author of confusion. There is so much to learn from this scripture. If nothing else, it should be warning that we trust no man.

I said it once, and I'll say it again—Jesus said to not judge because whatever judgement we judge, we will also be judged but to consider ourselves equal lest we find ourselves in a familiar situation.

One thing that I did notice about the false prophet is that he was careful not to say that it was the Lord who told him to invite the man of God to go home with him for dinner. "Even the demons believe and tremble," says the scripture. He had that much fear of

God. God is a mysterious God, who can know him. He used that false prophet to prophesy a word of truth to the man of God of his impending tragic demise for disobeying God's word to come back with the false prophet to his house.

Maybe, you're thinking like I am—why did the man of God who had been used of God, led by God, knew the voice of God, why not just ask himself, "How come my God didn't speak to me himself, why did he go through a third person using an angel? Too many red flags to just follow blindly to a total stranger.

And interestingly, that false prophet, upon hearing the fulfillment of the prophesy mourned the death of the man of God saying "Alas, my brother," and recovering his body had him buried in his own grave with instructions to his sons to be buried next to the man of God upon his own death. Now it would seem that he had no ill will of maliciousness for the man of God personally, however, the enemy of all righteousness did though. And the false prophet will still have to stand before God to give an account for the role he played in Satan's plot to kill God's prophet, regardless of what I might think or any other human summation and God will judge him, accordingly and righteously. Amen.

Keep in mind, King Jeroboam was so angry at the man of God that he would've destroyed him if he could of for prophesying against the altar at Bethel. People in high places do not like their wickedness exposed. This was a mighty man of God who boldly and bravely preached what thus said the Lord. A man who could be further used in a mighty way in the kingdom of heaven and the kingdom of God. Therefore, he had become a very real threat against Satan and his kingdom. This is a perfect example of "The kingdom of heaven suffers violence and the violent taketh it by force." Amen.

Notes

Chapter Sixteen

God's Modus Operandi

God wants us to live victorious Christian lives. But for us to win our daily battles, we need to follow the One who leads us.

Read more at https://www.whatchristianswanttoknow.com/battles-in-the-bible-7-you-need-to-know-about/#ixzz85f6nPjHN.

Modus operandi—a particular way or method of doing something, especially one that is characteristic or well-established:

Modus operandi is a Latin term used in English-speaking circles to describe an individual's or group's habitual way of operating, which forms a discernible pattern. The term is primarily used when discussing criminal behavior, but it is not exclusively uttered in this context. Modus operandi can also be defined as a specific method of operation.

For example, military strategists refer to an enemy's modus operandi when predicting the next threatening move in an armed conflict. Synonymous with the term *operating mode*, modus operandi is routinely shortened to the initials MO" in both written and verbal usage.

Utilizing Modus Operandi

An enemy's MO can be used by security experts to prevent an attack while it's still in the preparation stages. Known as "predictive profiling," this behavior is an extension of an MO that was developed by Israeli security forces in an effort to predict terrorist behavior, based on observing a group's or an individual's behavioral patterns.

"He's a God who never changes" (Heb. 13:8).

Jesus Christ is the same yesterday, today, and forever.

He has always existed and always will. He has no beginning and no ending.

"I am Alpha and Omega, the beginning and the ending, saith the Lord, which is, and which was, and which is to come, the Almighty" (Rev. 1:8).$

God is sovereign.

"Thus saith the Lord the King of Israel, and his redeemer the Lord of hosts; I am the first, and I am the last; and beside me there is no God" (Is. 44:6).

"See now that I, even I, am he, and there is no god with me: I kill, and I make alive; I wound, and I heal: neither is there any that can deliver out of my hand" (Deut. 32:39).

God is almighty.

El Shaddai. "And when Abram was ninety years old and nine, the Lord appeared to Abram, and said unto him, I am the Almighty God" (Gen. 17:1).

The omnipotence, omniscience, and omnipresence of God the three "omni" attributes of God characterize him as all-powerful, all-knowing, and everywhere present.

He is God of battle and war. Consider Deuteronomy 7:9. God gave the Israelite a promised land filled with milk and honey (Exod. 3:8). And I am come down to deliver them out of the hand of the Egyptians, and to bring them up out of that unto a land flowing with milk and honey.

But they had to go in and fight to possess it with the Lord fighting with them and on their behalf, giving them victory. Joshua and his forces attacked the land and killing all the Canaanite inhabitants and taking over the land.

"For thou art a holy people unto the Lord thy God: the Lord thy God hath chosen thee to be a special people unto himself, above all people that are upon the face of the earth.

"The Lord did not set his love upon you, nor choose you, because ye were more in number than any people; for ye were the fewest of all people.

"But because the Lord loved you, and because he would keep the oath which he had sworn unto your fathers, hath the Lord brought you out with a mighty hand, and redeemed you out of the house of bondmen, from the hand of Pharaoh king of Egypt" (Deut. 7:6–8). So are we now likewise in this dispensation under the new covenant. "But you are a chosen generation, a royal priesthood, a holy nation, his own special people, that you may proclaim the praises of him who called you out of darkness into his marvelous light" (1 Pet. 2:9). Who once were not a people but are now the people of God,

who had not obtained mercy but now have obtained mercy.

"The earth is the Lord's and the fullness thereof and them that dwell therein and that settles it" (Ps. 24: 1). Satan may be the prince of the power of the air (Eph. 2:2), but remember who the Creator of us all is and the creature can never be greater than its creator.

We know that we have a place in heaven, because Jesus said he's gone to prepare a place for us that where he is we may be with him there are many mansions there. "Heaven is his throne, and earth is his footstool" (Is. 66:1).

We must develop this mentality that all things are ours according to the Word of God (1 Cor. 3:22).

Notes

Chapter Seventeen

This Is War

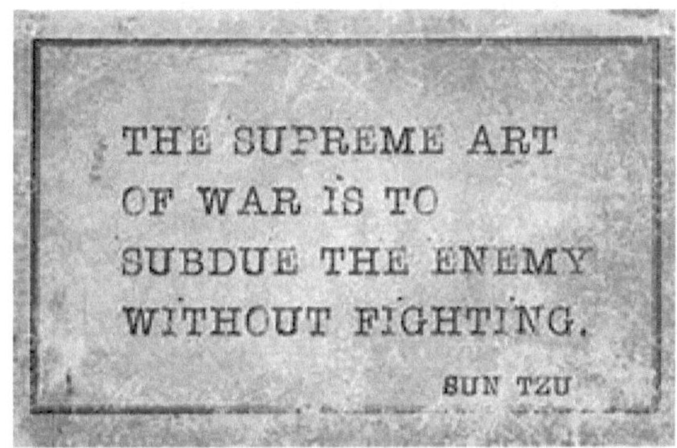

"For the weapons of our warfare are not carnal but mighty through God to the pulling down of stronghold" (2 Cor. 10:4).

The phrase "the weapons of our warfare are not carnal" is a biblical reference from 2 Corinthians 10:4. It means that the spiritual weapons used by Christians to fight against evil are not physical weapons but rather spiritual ones. These spiritual weapons include prayer, faith, love, hope, and the word of God. The passage emphasizes that Christians should not rely on their own strength or abilities to fight against evil, but rather on the power of God.

"But God hath chosen the foolish things of the world to confound the wise; and God hath chosen the weak things of the world to confound the things which are mighty" (1 Cor. 1:27).

For example, let's look at Jeremiah 9:17–20.

"Thus saith the Lord of hosts, 'Consider ye, and call for the mourning women, that they may come; and send for cunning women, that they may come.'

"And let them make haste and take up a wailing for us that our eyes may run down with tears, and our eyelids gush out with waters. For a voice of wailing is heard out of Zion, how are we spoiled! We are greatly confounded because we have forsaken the land, because our dwellings have cast us out.

"Yet hear the word of the Lord, O ye women, and let your ear receive the word of his mouth, and teach your daughters wailing, and everyone her neighbor lamentation."

This definitely would likely seem to be ludicrous in a war or a battle! The question that most likely will arise is "Why would you call for women to cry and to wail now for what have befallen God's people who are taken into captivity by their enemies because of their intentional disobedience to the commandments and oracles of God?" Now that the consequences for their sins have caused grief and sufferings, prayers with crying and wailing are offered up to God for their forgiveness, deliverance, and restoration for his goodness and mercy and grace.

Notes

Chapter Eighteen

The Early Crusades

"The kingdom of heaven suffers violence and the violent take it by force" (Matt. 11:12).

And from the days of John the Baptist, until now, the kingdom of heaven suffereth violence, and the violent take it by force.

The Crusades were a series of religious wars initiated, supported, and sometimes directed by the Christian Latin Church in the period. The best known of these military expeditions are those to the Holy Land in the period between 1095 and 1291 that were intended to conquer Jerusalem and its surrounding area from Muslim rule. Beginning with the First Crusade, which resulted in the conquestof Jerusalem in 1099, dozens of military campaigns were organized, providing a focal point of European history for centuries. Crusading declined rapidly after the fifteenth century (from Wikipedia, the free encyclopedia).

Were the Crusades successful?

The First Crusade, called in response to a request for help from the Byzantine emperor Alexius Comnenus, was astonishingly successful. The Crusaders conquered Nicaea (in Turkey) and Antioch, and then went on to seize Jerusalem, and they established a string of Crusader-ruled states. However, after the Muslim leader Zangī captured one of them, the Second Crusade, called in response, was defeated at Dorylaeum (near Nicaea) and failed in an attempt to conquer Damascus.

The Third Crusade, called after the sultan Saladin conquered the Crusader state of Jerusalem, resulted in the capture of Cyprus and the successful siege of Acre (now in Israel), and Richard I's forces defeated those of Saladin at the Battle of Arsūf and at Jaffa. Richard signed a peace treaty with Saladin allowing Christians access to Jerusalem.

The Fourth Crusade—rather than attacking Egypt, then the center of Muslim power—sacked the Byzantine Christian city of Constantinople. None of the following Crusades were successful. The capture of Acre in 1291 by the Māmluk sultan al-Ashraf Khalil marked the end of Crusader rule in the Middle East.

The Crusades were organized by western European Christians after centuries of Muslim wars of expansion.

Their primary objectives were to stop the expansion of Muslim states, to reclaim for Christianity the Holy Land in the Middle East, and to recapture territories that had formerly been Christian. Many participants also believed that undertaking what they saw as holy war was a means of redemption and a way of achieving expiation of sins (from Encyclopedia Brittanica).

Were the crusades organized by the church? Yes! According to two sources from livescience.com and En.wikipedia.com.

The Crusades were a series of religious wars initiated in 1095 by the Roman Catholic Church. They continued, in various forms, for centuries. The most well-known Crusades took place between 1095 and 1291 in the Near East, where European Christian armies attempted to recover the city of Jerusalem from Islamic rule.

In the twenty-first century this is a much-discussed topic and with it comes the many different commentators who have offered various explanations to what the interpretation is or the meaning of "The kingdom of heaven suffers violence and the violent take it by force."

Throughout the New Testament, terms as "fight the good fight of faith," "put on the whole armor of God," "shield of faith," "sword of the spirit" are terms describing battle, fighting, war, death, and violence but done in the spirit of the Holy Ghost.

But many scholars will tell you that God is a God of peace and love and that he opposes any form of violence. Then what about the Israelites that had been given a land that flowed with milk and honey? A plush land rich with water and streams. A land called Canaan, which was inhabited by unbelievers and Gentiles. At the same time, many scholars have called The Conquest of Canaan a holy war.

You should definitely read the writings from this link, "Why Did God Command the Invasion of Canaan in the Book of Joshua?" (bibleproject.com), for clarity and understanding. Above all pray, pray, and pray some more to the God that will open our understanding to all truth. Because one thing he's not is a God of confusion. Amen.

And I guarantee you, he will answer your prayer when you ask from a sincere heart and mind and soul. I know some may ask, "Why does God allow bad things to happen to good people?" I look at a statement in the Bible in response to that question in Psalm 51:5. It was the sin of humanity and the disobedience to keep God's commandments that keep us from the life he has always desired to give us. Behold, I was shaped in iniquity; and in sin did my mother conceive me. God loves every soul, and every soul belongs to him.

It's the sin, iniquity, idolatry, and the transgression that is committed by humanity that God despises, not his creation. He desires that none should perish but that all come to repentance and salvation.

For the wages of sin is death, but the gift of God is eternal life. No unrepentant soul can enter heaven unless he is born again of water and spirit (John 3:3) regardless of self-righteous acts of good- ness. At times, things do happen to good people that we will never understand or comprehend, but let's not blame God because he sees everything the good bad and the ugly, and he is the judge of us all and he have said, "Vengeance is mine, saith the Lord." My family experienced the death of a loved one unexpectedly and suddenly. I was very close with this family member, whom I admired, loved, and thought the world of.

I was newly born again, less than a year and new in the faith, when death came. I might mention we were both in our twenties at the time and only a year apart. I excitedly share my new birth experience, the scripture, and Jesus Christ as Redeemer and Savior. Fasting for my loved one was on my list to do when I received the news of their passing.

I was in total shock for days, and I questioned God. I blamed him because I asked him how he could let that happen when he knew that I was about to go on a fast for their deliverance of spiritual strongholds and salvation.

I had so many mixed emotions going on inside of me because my heart was totally broken into pieces. But because of his unconditional love and ability to know and try the reigns of the hearts of us all, he bore that pain with me and healed me so that I could go on to fulfill my own destiny. To me, the epitome of a good person died too soon.

We are in this world, but not of it. Not all men believe and that is something that my readers will all have to realize. Are these questions ever legitimating. "Their life was just beginning, why do the innocent have to be victimized, and evil men continue to prosper in their deeds?" We have the scriptures and the Holy Ghost to lead us, guide, and comfort us along this tedious journey. Hallelujah and praise God. 2 Thessalonians 3:1-5

"Finally, brethren, pray for us, that the word of the Lord may have free course, and be glorified, even as it is with you. And that we may be delivered from unreasonable and wicked men for all men have not faith. But the Lord is faithful, who shall stablish you, and keep you from evil. And we have confidence in the Lord touching you, that ye both do and will do the things which we command you. And the Lord direct your hearts into the love of God, and into the patient waiting for Christ" (2 Thess. 3:1–5).

That is exactly what he did for me, amid the storm and while I was in my grieving process. God stablished me in the faith and kept my foot from falling. Not only that but from that evil and wicked one, Satan the devil. When we doubt and question God about things that we could never see or understand, we're allowing temptation to enter our hearts, and we are then vulnerable to all sorts of inconceivable falsehoods. Watch and pray always. Build yourselves up on your most holy faith, having done all to stand, stand on. Amen.

The anti-Christ goes to and fro seeking who he may devour. His only mission or purpose is to kill, steal, and destroy. Operating in those who deny that Jesus Christ is the son of God, Savior, and redeemer to all who will be saved. As the time draws near for the second coming of Jesus, the wickedness of men and hearts have waxed colder.

But when I look at that verse, "The kingdom of heaven suffers violence and the violent takes it by force," then approach the statement with an analytical angle word by word. What is and where is the kingdom of heaven? "And God said, let there be a firmament in the midst of the waters, and let it divide the waters from the waters

"And God made the firmament, and divided the waters, which were under the firmament from the waters which were above the firmament: and it was so. And God called the firmament Heaven. And the evening and the morning were the second day" (Gen. 1:6–8).

Take a step back and see. And the Spirit of God moved upon the face of the waters. Even before the firmament of heaven, there was God; the Creator of all things, seen and unseen. God's kingdom is the only kingdom that matters because he's Sovereign. He said that his Kingdom is not of this world (John 18:36). Christ's kingdom is spiritually active in the world today, and one day he will return to physically reign on the earth in millennial glory (Rev. 11:15; 20:6).

His kingdom exists in the hearts of believers, where he is undisputed king and sovereign Lord. We can trace the origins of everything back to the book of Genesis. Bu, one thing is for sure, God is too big to fathom or grasp the fullness of him, and we'll never know it all or understand it all. His ways or far above our ways as the sky is above the earth.

Here we see that heaven is a creation of God, and therefore, it is his kingdom, and he is King and Ruler and Sovereign over everything because he's creator of it all.

However, we live in a time where the body of Christ recognizes that we battle in the spirit realm to maintain peace, harmony, love, and the freedom to worship freely the Almighty God. This war that we fight is not physical but spiritual to bring down spiritual demonic forces that work in unbeliever's hearts and who are anti-Christ to the work of Satan to annihilate the body of Christ.

However, we do recognize the fact for the need for actual military men and women to go into battle in the natural realm as well because in the book of Ecclesiastes 3:8 reads, "A time to love, and a time to hate, a time of war, and a time of peace."

So it is extremely important that we pray for the United States and our military forces that do go into battle on land, sea, and air to keep us free from foreign enemies and evil dictators that will steal our freedom to worship the one true God in Christ Jesus as well as for our sisters and brothers all over the world that are in the body of Christ.

The only reason that the children of God in biblical times were held in captivity as slaves in their own countries, as well as other countries, one being Babylon, Egypt, Persia, Greece, and Rome, is because of their constant idolatry and disobedience to the oracles of God. We must continue to obey "what thus saith the Lord" to maintain our freedom to worship God openly and without the threat of evil men and unbeliever. That we pray for continued freedom from communist countries, as the likes the Republic of China. Amen.

Make no mistake about it, the Church of God is definitely threatened and suffers violence as we've seen in recent years, both spiritually and naturally.

Church attacks fly under media, political radar Catholics frustrated.

The US Conference of Catholic Bishops reported ninety-three incidents as of August 24 in twenty-eight states since May 2020, including "arson, statues beheaded, limbs cut, smashed, and painted."

FBI data underscores rising threat to places of worship.

Monsey stabbing and Texas church shooting join long list of attacks on faith communities, which surged by 34.8 percent between 2014 and 2018.

In my opinion, these statistics are extremely alarming and should cause great concern to the kingdom of God and his Saints, because for the most part, many are clueless to what is going on right under our noses.

We're so unaware and asleep to what's hidden in plain sight. "We're destroyed for lack of knowledge." Jesus said, "My people are destroyed for lack of knowledge but let him ask." If any of you lack wisdom, let him ask of God, that giveth to all men liberally, and upbraideth not; and it shall be given him. This means WAR on a whole another level (Hosea 4:6 and James 1:5).

FBI hate crime statistics show that incidents in churches, synagogues, temples, and mosques increased 34.8 percent between 2014 and 2018, the last year for which FBI data is available.

However, the database wouldn't include the most recent attacks that have refocused attention on the security vulnerabilities at religious institutions.

Who can answer this type of violence or explain it in any other words than hate crimes against the believers of Jesus from the anti-Christ and Satan himself whose only purpose is to kill, steal, and destroy the people of God in any way that he can and does. We need to be the *watchers* for our generation, saints of the Most High God. The Bible teaches that we're to watch and pray.

Clearly the anti-Christ is on a rampage because Satan know that he's on a timeline, and it's winding down. He knows the Bible and the prophesy of God is true that foretells at the end the Church of God will triumph victoriously over the enemy. He knows that he is a defeated foe; we're the only ones that need to be reminded of this truth. In the end, *we will win.*

Faith is the substance of things hoped for, the evidence of things not seen. While it may appear to be alarming and as though the world has gone completely on the dark side, let not your heart be trouble, you believe in God, Jesus said, believe also in me. In my father's house there are many mansions.

If it were not so, I would have told you so, "I go to prepare a place for you, that where I am you may be also and if I go, I will come again to receive you unto me" (John 14:3). Be not weary in well doing but be steadfast in the faith and unmovable because our heavenly father will not allow us to suffer more than we can bear and with every temptation he will make a way of escape for us. If we will but only believe and trust him. Amen.

He has not left us comfortless but has given us his Holy Spirit that lives within us to strengthen and comfort us in the time of trouble. Jesus gives us these encouraging words, he says, "Come unto me, all ye that labor and are heavy laden, and I will give you rest. Take my yoke upon you and learn of me; for I am meek and lowly in heart: and ye shall find rest unto your souls" (Matt. 11:28-29).

However, as Saints of the Most High God and as His children, we must and we should after receiving the news of all the alarming attacks against believers and churches, react accordingly. How do we do that and what should we be doing.

We must really work and study to show ourselves a workman that needed not to be ashamed according to the word of God (2 Tim. 2:15). It's not enough to merely repeat words that we learned when we were first born again. But now as mature Christians, our words need to be backup with power and authority. Fight the good fight of faith literally means *fight*. Yes, we will definitely get tired, but we have a refuge in Jesus Christ our Lord.

Okay, now with all that said, what is the body of Christ to do with all this information? Somewhere in the scripture, it is said. "Show me your faith, and I will show you my faith by my works."

We are a work in progress. I am mindful more and more every day that I must practice entering into his rest until it's as common as brushing my teeth before bed and the first thing in the morning. It will become a learned behavior. A lawyer practices law, a surgeon practices medicine. It's an ongoing lesson an ongoing practice so to speak, there is no graduation before we come to the fulness of Christ Jesus.

"That we henceforth be no more children, tossed to and fro, and carried about with every wind of doctrine, by the sleight of men, and cunning craftiness, whereby they lie in wait to deceive" (Eph. 4:14). And be renewed in the spirit of your mind.

If we are longing for that peace that passes all understanding (Phil. 4:7) and the peace of God, which passeth all understanding, shall keep your hearts and minds through Christ Jesus. I've come to understand that anything outside of the Holy Ghost is generic and is only temporary. Jesus said, "We will find rest for our souls." It's what we all long for.

"Oh, what peace we often forfeit, oh, what needless pain we bear, all because we do not carry everything to God in prayer." Those are the lyrics to an ole hymnal, and it still resonates today in my heart, soul, and mind. What a friend we have In Jesus. What a privilege it is to carry everything to God in prayer.

What a loving Father and friend that we have in King Jesus. He's literally there for us to take the burdens and labors off our shoulders. In other words, in Matthew 11, "I will be your strength and your bridge over troubled waters, I will help you to carry your cross as Simon of Cyrene helped me." When the road gets rugged, I'll be your shoulder to lean on. That your labor is not in vain. But if we don't take the initiative to obtain that privilege to learn from him and to find that peace unto our very soul, then as the scripture forewarns us. "Unless the Lord builds the house, we labor in vain." Just think about what this means for a minute.

To have the privileged opportunity of the blessed restoration of how things were before the fall. Glory and hallelujah. The magnitude of such profound love that is uncompromising and so perfect is truly incomprehensible. It literally blows my mind. I've experienced the power of his love time and time again throughout my life's journey. I live and breathe it every second, and we don't fear death because to be absent from the body is to present with the Lord. It's through death that we enter into that eternal life with him.

Jesus Christ said to man that was alongside him on the cross, and within minutes before their deaths, "Today shall you be with me in paradise." Wow! What a mighty God we serve. In any given moment, he's in control. He's a man's man. Check him out.

To the human view, it's like we're both going to be buried in the ground and you say this! But the man on the cross was not thinking through a carnal mind but through the eyes of a man who saw Jesus as the Savior and the Redeemer of all mankind who gave his life freely and who would rise from the dead in three days with all power and authority sitting on the right hand of God. Amen.

Notes

Chapter Nineteen

The Conclusion of the Matter

Be strong in the Lord and in the power of his might, because in him we are more than conquerors remembering that above all else; that he has not given us the spirit of fear but the spirit of love, power, and a sound mind. The Bible teaches that one will put a thousand to flight and two ten thousand to flight Deuteronomy 32:30, "How should one chase a thousand, and two put ten thousand to flight, except their Rock had sold them, and the Lord had shut them up?"

We have benefits and resources available to us through the Holy Ghost that we have yet to realize if we were but to trust the author and finisher of our faith. It will be virtually impossible for us fail heaven and eternal life will be ours. Amen

Do we know what these real details are? It means that our hope is in Jesus Christ the risen King. "It means that hope maketh not ashamed. Therefore being justified by faith, we have peace with God through our Lord Jesus Christ by whom also we have access by faith into this grace wherein we stand and rejoice in hope of the glory of God. And not only so, but we glory in tribulations also: knowing that tribulation worketh patience; and patience, experience; and experience, hope, and hope maketh not ashamed; because the love of God is shed abroad in our hearts by the Holy Ghost which is given unto us (Rom. 5:1–5). Keep the faith. What is faith? it's the substance of things hoped for, the evidence of things not seen. Blessed is the man who believes and have not seen than the man who only believes when it's looking them squarely in the face.

I can't say this enough because it must permeate deep into the soul of man, "We have peace with God." The Bible says in Isaiah 26: 3, "Thou wilt keep him in perfect peace, whose mind is stayed on thee: because he trusteth in thee."

We're guaranteed of overcoming the world and the wiles of the devils because if God is for us, who then can be against us (Rom. 8). And that is totally real and true because I've experienced the divine intervention of angels for myself on more than one occasion. "For he shall give his angels charge over thee, to keep thee in all thy ways" (Ps. 91:11). A militant warrior is always armored up with the whole armor of God. Change your lifestyle as more than conquerors.

Notes

It's her passion to write creative stories. She loves to write about suspense and drama that will spark her readers' imagination. Anything involving words, she loves. The word game scrabble is another passion of hers. It challenges her and provokes her to learn new words every day. There is not a day that goes by that she doesn't play scrabble. Her mind craves learning, and she's currently learning and practicing another language, French. She's more than one year in of learning French, and it's such a beautiful and exotic language to her.